THE ULTIMATE PARIS GUIDE

Your valuable trip Companion

by Cathryn Sparks

UUGuides™

This publication is designed to provide accurate and authoritative information with regard to the subject matter covered. It is sold with the understanding that the publisher and the author are not engaged in rendering legal, accounting, or other professional advice. If legal advice or other expert assistance is required, the services of a competent professional person should be sought.

Table of Contents

What's special about this guide?

The travel guide you are holding was designed to offer you all the information that you will need if you are planning a trip to Paris, while at the same time being practical and in a normal size, since 400 or 500 page books are not easy to carry or search while on a trip. We believe that we have achieved to create a guide for Paris that is on the golden line between information and size.

The writer, Cathryn Sparks, is an urban travel specialist with experience in trip planning and multi-cultural sociological analysis. An avid traveler herself, she has visited many great cities of the world, and is happy to channel all the information and knowledge she has about them through her books. All her books are written in cooperation with local experts.

By buying this book, either in electronic or in printed form, you automatically gained access to the *"Paris download zone"* section of our website www.uuguides.com, with many useful info, like the Paris city, metro and train maps, museum plans, but most importantly an interactive route map, that accompanies this book, with detailed routes on Google maps, for every day of your trip, plus location, information and photos of all the important attractions of Paris. You will find the password and instructions on how to enter "Paris download zone" in the respective chapter of this book. Moreover, you will find instructions on how to get a *complete French phrasebook* absolutely for free.

Let me quickly introduce you to what this book will offer you. To start with, it will help you decide the best time of the year to visit Paris according to your personal tastes and your expectations from this trip. It will also help you decide which part of the city is the best for you to look for accommodation. Detailed information on safety is also provided in the respective chapter, in order to protect you from booking that very nice and cheap hotel you found on the internet, but located in a shady neighborhood. It will also protect you from various types of scams that you will most likely come across within the streets of Paris (there is even a detailed catalog of scams and how they work!). An "important things to know" chapter concludes the general knowledge anyone should have before visiting Paris.

When you arrive in Paris, this guide will help you get to the city center and to your hotel by choosing the best transportation means to suit your needs and budget. Detailed maps of the transportation system are provided in the download zone.

Once you start your adventure in Paris, you will find everything about Paris's attractions, a selection of the ones you must see, but this guide goes even further by providing a list of the major free attractions, for those of you that travel on a budget. Apart from the great monuments and attractions though, Paris is also a very romantic city, and a cruise on the River Seine is bound to be one of the most romantic moments that you will ever have. Our guide explains how the cruise system works and what you need to do in order to book a cruise from the internet before even going to Paris!

Other important chapters include French gastronomy and what you definitely need to taste, from street food to sophisticated French delicacies, the transportation system and how it works, and of course shopping and the best places to shop according to your tastes and budget, plus a lot more useful info, all provided in this guide.

This is not an ordinary travel guide, since it contains innovations that can make your perfect trip even more perfect! Technology today is a big help, and most people use smartphones. There are some great apps that will make your trip to Paris easier and more fun, and we present them to you- always trying to suggest free apps. Except from all the above, we have also carefully created a detailed itinerary for you, in order to organize your trip in the best possible way. You will find this itinerary in the respective chapter of this book, but you will also find an interactive form of the Itinerary in the download zone of our Website www.uuguides.com, by using the password that you will find in this book.

Last but not least, you can get a complete French phrasebook for free. You can find all appropriate info in the respective chapter, "French Phrasebook".

How to use this guide

We have designed this guide to be as simple and practical as possible, and we have tried to organize and plan as many things as we can for you. We believe that we have created a very easy-to-use guide, with all the information that you will need, but in the same time it is not a usual guide. We have incorporated many innovative things with the help of technology, and we believe that your experience from your trip to Paris will be ameliorated significantly with the help of our tools.

In order to fully exploit this guide, you need to do some reading before going to Paris. Chapters on when to go, how to get to Paris, Paris neighborhoods, safety concerns, important things to know and useful apps contain information that will affect your preparations on your upcoming trip. All other chapters can be read while in Paris, but we suggest you read the whole book before landing. Also, we recommend that you access "Paris download zone" before visiting Paris as well.

The detailed Itinerary we have created for you, focuses on visiting all must-see Paris attractions within 5 days. There is an extension of 2 more days for those that are going to stay for 7 days. In case you stay longer, you can just loosen the schedule, or have a couple of days just strolling around Paris's lovely streets. Note that we have tried to include most important Paris attractions in the first 3 days, convenient for those of you that are going to stay for less than 5 days. Don't forget to also use the interactive Itinerary that we have created for you. It shows your everyday routes on Google maps, with perks like zooming in or out, moving the entire map, seeing road names and distances etc.

Concerning the smartphone apps, we have divided them according to the operating system you might have, android apps in case you own android smartphones and iOS apps in case you own an iPhone or iPad.

Paris in a few words

Paris is the capital and most populous city of France with more than 12 million inhabitants in the Paris region, almost 20% of France's total population. It is situated on the Seine River, in the north of the country, in the "Paris Region" or "Region Parisienne". Paris was founded in the 3rd century BC by Celtic people, and, by the end of the 12th century became the largest city of the western world. You may also know it as the "City of light" ("La Ville Lumiere" in French). This nickname derives from two different facts, the first being Paris' leading role during the age of enlightenment, and the second that Paris was one of the first European cities to adopt gas street lighting. Inhabitants of Paris are known as "Parisians" ("Parisiens" in French). Paris receives more than 22 million tourists every year, which makes it one of the world's top tourist destinations. The majority of tourists come from the United States, UK, Germany, Italy, Japan, Spain and China.

Paris is divided into 20 administrative districts called "arrondissements". Some of them are better to stay at, safer and with many more things to do, while other are less safe and more obscure from the places most tourists move. Later in this guide, I will present all 20 arrondissements to you, and give you some basic information about each one of them.

Paris is known for many things. You will be able to view the city from 986 ft high on one of the world's most iconic monuments, the Eiffel tower. You can drink a cafe or a glass of red wine at its second floor cafeteria, gazing at "Arc de Triomphe", "Champ de Mars" or "Les Invalides". This will be one of the most beautiful experiences of your life. Sipping a glass of wine at Trocadero, looking at the Eiffel tower at night with all its lights twinkling for 5 minutes at the start of each hour is also a wonderful experience.

You will also get to see an amazing array of art collections, from ancient Greece, Rome, Egypt, Persia, Middle East and many other places around the world. "Sully", "Richelieu" and "Denon", the three wings of the Louvre museum with its extensive and priceless collections, will travel you to many places and times. From Pharaonic Egypt to the Renaissance and from classical Greece to Napoleonic times and the Rococo period, Louvre will astonish you with its splendor and diversity. Mona Lisa by Leonardo Da Vinci, Venus de Milo, Victory of Samothrace, the colossal statue of Ramses II, Captive (dying slave) by Michelangelo and the Napoleon's apartments are only some of the masterpieces that you will have the opportunity to admire in the Louvre Museum.

Cruising the waters of the Seine River during the daylight is great, but during night, dazzled by Paris's lights and their reflections on the water, admiring the greatness of the Eiffel tower from right beneath it while drinking mulled warm wine during winter or white wine during summer will be an experience that you will never forget. If you plan on doing that along with your spouse or your better half, it might be the most romantic thing of your life.

Other interesting places await you; the Avenue des Champs-Elysees with its posh designer shops and galleries, Monmarte with its street artists ready to capture your image on canvas, Hotel des Invalides-which is the resting place of Napoleon Bonaparte, St-Germain-des-Pres- the most classically Parisian neighborhood and lots of museums, including medieval ones, the Notre Dame Cathedral, the Sacre Coeur, flea markets, shopping malls, bakeries, restaurants, monuments, city walks and much more. I will give you information about all these places and much more in this guide.

Paris is the city of romance, city of love and red wine, city of lights and French cuisine, city of culture and Parisian fashion. Whatever your interests are, Paris will surely amaze you and find its way into your heart for the rest of your life.

When to go

A dilemma in many people's minds is which time of the year is best to travel to Paris. Most, without a second thought, would say spring and summer, because the weather is good, days are longer and most of the tourists visit Paris during these periods. I would say that Paris is magical all year long, and it can offer different vacation experiences in different times of the year. It depends on what one wants when traveling to Paris. Each season has its pros and cons, which I will describe right below to help you choose the best season to suit your personal tastes!

Spring

It is usually a bit chilly in Paris until the end of April, but still, spring is one of the best seasons of the year to visit Paris. You won't have to face Paris's hot summer or bitter winter. The days are long, ideal for endless walks and the blooming flowers and trees give a colorful beauty to the city and a perfect setting to your photos. It is the best time of the year to visit its many parks and gardens, like the Jardin du Luxembourg, or take short, day trips outside the city, for instance to the Versailles, which during spring are most beautiful, with the magnificent gardens a must-see attraction themselves. Locals have the best mood in spring as well, and the friendlier atmosphere is ideal for interacting. Most cafes and restaurants have tables outdoors, and spring is the best time to enjoy a cup of coffee or a glass of wine, while watching the Eiffel tower or the Notre-Dame Cathedral.

Visiting Paris in spring also has its drawbacks though. Airplane and train fares as well as hotel prices rise along with the temperature, and might not be feasible for some to visit Paris at this time of the year. Hotel occupancy rates peak in the spring and summer, and it might be difficult to find proper accommodation, even if you are willing to pay more that you originally planned. Same goes for airport and train tickets, and it is best to book all the above at least 5 months in advance, if you are traveling at spring or summer. Even if you find the tickets and hotel though, you must be prepared for long queues in Paris's top attractions such as the Eiffel tower, the Louvre, Notre Dame, etc. To give you a taste, the average waiting time for the Eiffel tower during spring and summer is 2.5 hours. Purchasing a Paris museum pass or ticket through the internet before going to Paris though will help you avoid those lines. Finding a seat in cafes and restaurants can also be an issue, at least near the top tourist attractions, but things get better a little further from them, where it's less crowded. Lastly, for those who have allergies or asthma, Paris tends to have high airborne pollen and pollution levels in the spring, so make sure you bring along all appropriate medications.

Summer

Summer days in Paris might get a bit hot, but the atmosphere remains fabulous. Outdoor music festivals like the Paris Street Music Festival (Fete de la Musique), many of which are for free, will offer you the greatest of times if you are a fan. Even a walk along the Seine during nighttime with the soft breeze caressing your face will make you feel renascent. The atmosphere is relaxed and carefree, making it an ideal time for picnics in Paris' elegant parks or across the banks of Seine. Most people in Paris during the summer will be tourists, since the locals tend to leave the city for their summer holidays, so this is a great opportunity to meet and interact with people from all over the world.

Some people might feel though that this lack of Parisians distorts their experience of Paris, since they don't have the opportunity to fully interact with the locals. Most people you communicate with are tourists as well, and even a number of stores remain closed for short periods of time, though, truth being told, the situation has become better during the last 5 years, since most stores remain open, and less Parisians leave the city during summer. What I mentioned in the spring section about expensive air and train tickets and high hotel prices applies during summer as well, accompanied by endless lines in most major attractions. The number of tourists during summer is roughly the same as in spring, which means Paris is full. Some think that at least the weather will compensate, but that is not the case in summer Paris, since the weather can be erratic and really unpredictable. Sudden bursts of rain or intense heat waves can ruin plans for outdoor activities, even a simple walk, and extreme heat can be dangerous for elderly or very young visitors, who should be prepared by always carrying appropriate supplies like water and by being dressed accordingly.

Autumn

While chill may be back in Paris in the autumn, the bright and crisp light of the morning will imprint some of the most beautiful images on your mind and you camera! Multi-colored falling leaves will also create a magical scenery for the romantic ones, who will grasp the opportunity to enjoy a "chocolat chaud" (hot chocolate) along with the locals, in a small and cozy Parisian cafe. Most locals will have returned from their summer vacations with their batteries fully charged, and will be trying to settle in to everyday life again, and also enjoying Paris themselves. So, this is the perfect time of the year to experience the truly Parisian everyday life, in a Paris that is preparing not for the next tourist wave, but for the upcoming winter. Furthermore, all tickets and hotel prices gradually drop starting from mid-October, depending of course on the weather.

Despite being uniquely beautiful, Paris in the autumn is darker than spring or summer, as the days grow smaller. Temperature gradually starts to drop and frequent rain showers make it more difficult to spend as many hours outdoors, as you would in the spring or summer. Also, you can't fully enjoy those exciting night walks along the Seine or other places of Paris, since it gets a bit chilly during the night. Added to the above, some tourist attractions might be closed during autumn and winter. Not the main ones, but mostly seasonal attractions. Also, you might come across a considerable number of public works, as they mostly take place during low seasons, and we all know how annoying this can be!

Winter

The greatest advantage of visiting Paris in the winter is that it is less crowded, so you won't have to face hordes of tourists when visiting attractions or when making restaurant reservations - with the exception of Christmas season. Visiting Paris during the Christmas season though is truly an amazing experience. Christmas lights and holiday displays elevate the city of lights to an even higher level of luminosity, and open Christmas markets offer unforgettable experiences to the little ones as well as couples. Outdoor ice skating is also available, plus Christmas at the Notre Dame or the Disneyland is magical. Winter is the most beautiful season to create unforgettable moments with your other half and/ or your family.

Short winter days and cold weather can sometimes be discouraging for walking outdoors and enjoying Paris's exquisite architecture and street life. Also, visiting certain monuments might not be as enjoyable, for example climbing at the top of the

Eiffel tower, since it gets frosty up there! Drinking a glass of mulled wine in the second floor of the tower though while admiring the magnificent panoramic view of Paris might compensate you for patiently enduring all that cold for that perfect selfie! Winter is best mostly for indoor activities, like visiting museums, drinking hot beverages in cafes and enjoying French cuisine in some of Paris' many restaurants. Certain attractions and stores are closed in the winter as well.

All in all there is no "best" time of the year to visit Paris; there is only what you want to experience in your travel. If you know what you want, you will surely be satisfied whichever season you choose to visit.

How to get to Paris

You can get to Paris by airplane, boat, train or car depending on where you are coming from. Travelers from other continents, like the Americas, of course mostly arrive on airplane.

Paris has two airports. International passengers touch down at Charles de Gaulle (CDG) airport to the northeast, while regional travelers usually land to Orly (ORY) airport, to the south. There is a third airport available, Beauvais Tille Airport (BVA), as an alternative aeronautical gateway to Paris. Beauvais is about an hour and fifteen minutes away from Paris by bus, in the Picardy countryside, and is mostly used by low cost airlines. There are direct flights to Paris from just about every country in the world. Charles de Gaulle and Orly airports are about 45 minutes from Paris's center if there is no traffic. You can use metro, bus or taxi to get to Paris's center. Metro and bus are quite cheap, at approximately 2 Euros per ticket, while cab will cost you about 25 Euros from Orly and 50 Euros from Charles de Gaulle. There is an extra charge of 1.50 Euros for suitcases and prices are higher between 7:00p.m.and 6:00 a.m. There are several bus lines connecting Charles De Gaul to central Paris but it is best to take the train which departs every 15 minutes between 5:30 a.m. and midnight from the airport station to Gare du Nord, Chatelet Les Halles and Luxembourg stations. From Orly, a shuttle bus will take you to the train, which departs every 15 minutes between 5:30 a.m. and 11:00 p.m. to Gare d'Austerlitz, St Michel/Notre Dame and Invalides stations. From Beauvais, taking the bus to Porte Maillot is a one way road. It will cost you around € 17.00 and it will take you to Porte Maillot Metro station, which is about 15 minutes from the center of Paris.

France also has one of the best rail networks in the world, with the renowned TGV as its centerpiece. Six major stations facilitate travelling in and out of Paris to and from neighboring cities and countries, including the U.K. (the train goes underwater). Travel time from London to Paris by train is 2 hours and 20 minutes. European travelers can also go to Paris by car. British travelers can get to France by boat (90 minute travel) and then drive or take a train to Paris.

Paris Neighborhoods

Tour Eiffel/Invalides

The 7th arrondisment is considered to be one of Paris's most upscale neighborhoods. From most of the 7th arrondissement's blocks there is an excellent view of the Eiffel Tower. Dominating the southwestern landscape of Paris, the Eiffel Tower did not receive a friendly welcome from Parisians when it first opened in 1889. Today though it is an iconic and beloved landmark, especially at night when its thousand twinkling lights sparkle at the start of every hour.

Other notable sights include Hotel des Invalides, a very large Baroque complex equipped with an impressive golden dome under which lies the extravagant tomb of Napoleon and, further down the river, the Palais Bourbon, seat of the National French Assembly, which is an homage to ancient Greek architecture. Nearby is the Musee du Quai Branly, the newest of the major museums in Paris, built by famous French architect Jean Nouvel, and featuring the indigenous art and collections of Africa, Asia Oceania and the Americas. There is also Musee Rodin, dedicated to the works of French sculptor Auguste Rodin, with its magnificent and extensive gardens, where many of Rodin's sculptures are displayed in natural settings.

To the east of the Eiffel Tower, walking along the Seine will lead you to Les Egouts, literally meaning "The Sewers", where you can tour and explore actual working sewers and learn all about their history, from their initial development in the late 14th century, to their modern structure. Also, nearby is the American Church with its well-known spire, which traces its roots back to 1814 and serves both the American expatriate community and a variety of other English- speaking people.

Another iconic landmark can be found close by, Pont Alexandre III, which is widely considered to be the most ornate and extravagant bridge in Paris. A marvel of 18th century engineering, it connects the Champs-Elysees quarter with those of the Invalides and Eiffel Tower, and is brimming with Art Nouveau lamps, cherubs, nymphs and winged horses. It was named after Tsar Alexander III in celebration of the Franco- Russian Alliance in 1892 and was inaugurated for the Exposition Universelle (Universal Exhibition) of 1900.

Louvre

The Louvre area roughly extends between the start of Rue Faubourg St-Honore to Paris's central Market, Les Halles. Rue Faubourg St-Honore is noted as one of the most luxurious and fashionable streets in the world, as almost every major fashion house has a strong presence there (it is home to the flagships of Lanvin and Hermes and headquarters of Lancome among others). It is also home to the Elysee Palace, official residence of the French president, the residence of many foreign ambassadors and numerous noted art galleries.

To the east end, you can find Les Halles de Paris, or simply Les Halles (pronounced le-al) the traditional central market of Paris, known as the "Belly of Paris", where for hundreds of years merchants came from all over to sell their goods. It was demolished in 1971 and replaced with the Forum des Halles, a modern shopping mall. The mall is undergoing a major reconstruction since 2010.

Between Faubourg St-Honore and Les Halles lie some of Paris's top attractions, including the world renowned Musee du Louvre and, just next to it, the magnificent Jardin des Tuileries. At the west corner of the garden, next to the Place de la Concorde, is the Musee de l' Orangerie, an art gallery of impressionist and post-impressionist paintings, where works by Paul Cezanne, Henri Matisse, Amedeo Modigliani, Pablo Picasso, Pierre-Auguste Renoir, and Henri Rousseau can be seen among others. The crown jewel of the museum though is indisputably the eight water lilies murals by Claude Monet.

In Place Colette lies the Comedie Francaise, one of the few state theatres in France. Founded by a decree of Louis XIV on August 8, 1680, thus with more than three centuries of history, it is the only state theatre to have its own troupe of actors. A colorful contrast to the neo-classical architecture of the Comedie-Francaise and the galleries that surround Place Colette is the Kiosque des Noctambules (Kiosk of the night-walkers). An art installation designed by Jean-Michel Othoniel, it is consisted of two cupolas, one representing the day, the other the night, made from Murano glass and aluminum. It was installed in 2000 to mark the centenary of Paris Metro and also serves as the entrance to the Palais Royal - Musee du Louvre station.

Just off Place Colette is the Palais-Royal and its romantic garden. Originally called the Palais-Cardinal, the palace was the personal residence of Cardinal Richelieu. Nearby is Galerie Vivienne, a beautifully restored 19th-century shopping gallery with exquisite decor.

Champs-Elysees

The Champs-Elysees is hands down the most famous avenue in Paris—and, perhaps, the entire world. Much like New York's Times Square or London's Piccadilly Circus, it is a Mecca for both travelers and locals, who proudly call it "la plus belle avenue du monde" (the most beautiful avenue of the world). It runs between Place de la Concorde and Place Charles de Gaulle and is known for its theatres, cafes and luxury shops. In recent years its character has radically changed with the introduction of global chain stores, a trend that at first did not sit well with the Parisians, who dubbed it "*banalisation*". However, this means that there are plenty of shops, cafes and restaurants to choose from, depending on your budget.

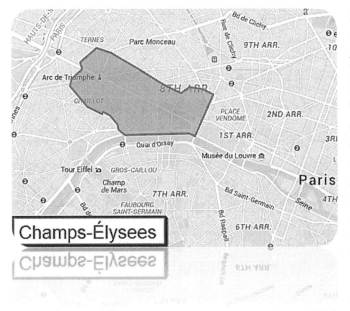

Champs-Élysees

Located at Place de Charles de Gaulle is the Arc de Triomphe, Napoleon's monument to...himself. The Arc de Triomphe is the linchpin of the "Axe historique" (historic axis), which is a sequence of monuments and grand thoroughfares on a route that runs from the courtyard of the Louvre to the Grande Arche de la Defense.

The lower part of the Champs, extending from the Place de la Concorde to the Rond-Point, runs through the Jardin des Champs-Elysees, a park which contains the exquisitely restored Grand Palais, where some of the city's grandest art exhibitions take place, the Petit Palais, with a free permanent art collection (and a beautiful garden cafe, that travels one back in time), the Theatre Marigny - originally built for the display of a panorama- and several restaurants, gardens and monuments. Also, the Elysee Palace (the official presidential residence) borders the park, but is not on the Avenue itself. Between here and Place du Trocadero, one can find several museums housed in some of Paris's most beautiful buildings. To start with, on Avenue du President Wilson is the Palais de Tokyo, a complex dedicated to modern and contemporary art. On its left wing is hosted the Palais de Tokyo/ Site de Creation Contemporaine, for the contemporary art lovers, and on its right wing lies the Musee d'Art Moderne de la Ville de Paris (Paris Museum of Modern Art), which contains a free permanent collection of more than 10,000 works from art movements of the 20th and 21st centuries, and runs Temporary exhibitions every six weeks. These two Art Nouveau buildings were inaugurated at the International Exhibition of Arts and Technology of 1937. Across the street, in a Renaissance- inspired palace, is located the Palais Galliera, a museum dedicated to fashion, where the visitor can observe the creative genius in fashion from the 18th century to present day. Farther on is the Musee Guimet, home to one of the largest collections of Asian art outside Asia. Finally, crowning Place du Trocadero at the Palais de Chaillot complex is the Cite de l'Architecture et du Patrimoine, a must visit for architecture lovers.

Montmartre

Montmartre nowadays has become almost too charming and touristy for its own good. There are still working artists here at Place du Tertre (though less than there used to be) and one of the best views of Paris can be seen from the top of the hill. That's why, mostly on weekends but all year-round, hundreds of visitors crowd these cobbled alleys and queue to visit Sacre-Coeur, the Basilica of the Sacred Heart of Paris, at the top of the hill. You can also attend one of the masses held there and enjoy the chorals of the Benedictine Sisters of the Sacred Heart of Montmartre.

Monmartre is at its best at nonpeak times, on a weekday, or in the morning or later in the evening. You can stroll around Place des Abbesses, with its rustic houses and narrow streets. At the beginning of the twentieth century, during the Belle Epoque, many artists had their studios or worked in or around Montmartre, including Salvador Dali, Camille Pissarro, Claude Monet, Piet Mondrian, Amedeo Modigliani, Pablo Picasso, Vincent van Gogh and Henri de Toulouse-Lautrec, whose paintings of the cancan dancers at the Moulin Rouge are now souvenir-shop fixtures. The Moulin Rouge in Place Blanche and the cabaret Au Lapin Agile are famous for their shows. Boulevard de Clichy was "the highway of the artists" during the Belle Epoque: Degas lived and died at No. 6, and Picasso lived at No. 11. In Monmartre can also be found the Cafe des Deux Moulins at 15 rue Lepic, the real-life cafe (with a remodeled look) where "Amelie" was filmed.

St-Germain-Des-Pres

A beautiful Parisian neighbouthood, increasingly popular with tourists, St-Germain-des-Pres has the full package: art galleries, famous cafes, designer boutiques, beautiful restaurants, and a fine selection of museums.

This quarter draws its name from the oldest church in Paris, St-Germain-des-Pres (founded in the 6th century). It has been a beehive of intellectuals since as early as the 17th century. Revolutionaries Jean-Paul Marat, Georges Danton, and Joseph-Ignace Guillotin lived here. Claude Monet and Auguste Renoir shared a studio at 20 rue Visconti, and Pablo Picasso lived in a room on Rue de Seine when he was young. After the Second World War, the neighbourhood became the center of intellectuals and philosophers, actors and musicians. Existentialism co-existed with jazz in the bars on the rue de Rennes. Jean-Paul Sartre, Simone de Beauvoir, Juliette Greco, Jean-Luc Godard, and Francois Truffaut were all there, talking about the meaning of existence at Cafe de Flore and Les Deux Magots.

Nearby, located in the 7th arrondissement, is one of Paris's top attractions, the Musee d'Orsay. Housed in the former Gare d'Orsay, a Beaux-Arts railway station built in the late 1890's, the museum is home to the largest collection of impressionist and post-impressionist masterpieces in the world. A visit to the Orsay should be planned with care, due to the all- year round long queues. Other notable sights include the Musee Delacroix, in Place Furstenburg, where the painter actually lived until his death on 1863 and contains a collection of his works and memorabilia, and the Eglise St-Sulpice, where you can see two impressive Delacroix frescoes.

St-Germain is one of the most enjoyable places in Paris to stroll. Make your way to the crossroads of Carrefour de Buci, filled with cafes, flower markets, and shops. Continue on to Rue de l'Ancienne Comedie, the first home of the legendary Comedie Francaise, and Rue St-Andre des Arts, where you can find the historic Cour du Commerce St-Andre (opposite No. 66), a picturesque cobbled passageway dotted with cafes and restaurants, including, halfway down on the left, the famous Le Procope, Paris' s oldest (opened in 1686!).

Do not miss out on a visit to the exquisite Jardin du Luxembourg, a garden that covers over 23 hectares, known for its lawns, beautiful tree-lined promenades, flowerbeds and for the picturesque Medici Fountain, built in 1620.

The Islands

Located at the very center of Paris, (quite literally, as Kilometre Zero is on the square facing the main entrance of Notre Dame Cathedral) are two tiny islands: Ile St-Louis and Ile de la Cite, linked to both banks of the Seine by a number of bridges. As they are in the center of Paris, those little islands are a great place to begin your visit, with some of the most picturesque views in Paris.

The Isle St- Louis, named after Louis IX (Saint Louis), King of France from 1226 to 1270, was originally used for the grazing of market cattle along with stocking wood. During the 17th century, King Louis XIII transformed it into an elegant neighborhood that has remained almost untouched to this day and is one of Paris's most authentic 17th- and 18th-century neighborhoods. It still is mostly a residential area, although several restaurants, hotels, shops, cafes and ice cream parlours can be found as well.

The Ile de la Cite is the center of Paris and the location where the medieval city was refounded. It is home to what is perhaps the most famous cathedral in the world, the magnificent Notre-Dame de Paris. The cathedral was built from 1163 to 1345 (!) on the site of a church dedicated to Saint Etienne, which in turn was erected over a sacred pagan site of Roman times, and is one of the three surviving medieval buildings on the island. The other two are the Conciergerie prison, where Queen Marie Antoinette awaited her execution in 1793, and the Sainte-Chapelle, a royal medieval gothic chapel and a beautiful example of gothic architecture, built between 1239 and 1248. It holds one of the most extensive on-site collections of 13th century stained glass anywhere in the world. Other important sights include the Palais de Justice, which encloses the Sainte- Chapelle, and The Memorial des Martyrs de la Deportation, dedicated to the 200,000 people deported from France to the Nazi concentration camps during the Second World War.

The Latin Quarter

For more than eight centuries now, the Latin Quarter remains the heart of student Paris. The oldest university in France, La Sorbonne, was founded here in 1257. The neighborhood derives its name from the Latin language, the language widely spoken in and around the University, since Latin was considered the language of learning in the Middle Ages in Europe. Today the area is known for its student life, lively atmosphere and bistros, bars, and shops.

Place St-Michel is considered the symbolic gateway to the quarter, with its 19th-century fountain depicting Saint Michael slaying the "demon". Today the fountain is a major meeting spot. The two main arteries running through the quarter are Boulevard St. Germain and Boulevard St. Michel, both very busy and with hundreds of small, twisty streets leading off them. The two streets intersect near the Musee de

Cluny, or the Musee national du Moyen Age (National Museum of the Middle Ages), a spectacular medieval building that combines Gothic and Renaissance elements, partially constructed on the remnants of the third century Gallo-Roman baths. The museum features an impressive collection of medieval artifacts and artwork and is famous for its six "The Lady and the Unicorn" (*La Dame a la licorne*) tapestries.

Walking up St. Michel after you pass the Cluny you will find some less crowded and more authentic bistros, and, of course, the Sorbonne, one of the first universities of the world, is only a few blocks away. If you keep walking and turn left off the rue Soufflot, you will eventually reach the Pantheon, looking out over all of Paris. The Pantheon, an early example of neoclassicism, with a facade modeled on the Pantheon of Rome, now functions as a secular mausoleum containing the remains of distinguished French citizens, including Rousseau, Voltaire, Victor Hugo, Louis Braille, Emile Zola, and Soufflot, its architect. It's in this building that the famous physicist, Foucault, proved the rotation of the earth by hanging his 67 meter pendulum from the dome in 1851.

Around the twisty streets behind the Pantheon, you will find Eglise Saint-Etienne du Mont, where on its front steps Gil is first whisked away to the world of the 1920s in the movie "Midnight in Paris".

Shop like a Parisian along Rue Mouffetard for one of the best selections of runny cheeses, fresh breads, and charcuterie. If you are on a budget, head back down toward the river, loop around the back of the Cluny Museum and investigate the small streets around. One of them is the extremely touristy rue de la Huchette, where you will find plenty of fast food joint, souvlaki shops, sushi, bakeries, Indian and 'authentic French cooking'. If you keep walking down the alley, cross the street and you will eventually come across the Shakespeare and Company Bookstore at rue de la Bucherie. One of the most interesting English language bookshops in Paris, the shop is a remake of the original bookstore founded by Sylvia Beach in the 1920s. It became a central point for expatriate Americans such as Pound, Hemmingway and the Irishman James Joyce. The benches and fountain outside the shop are a great place to sit and muse at Notre Dame across the river.

Le Marais

The Marais is a fascinating district with a fascinating history. It's full of small crooked medieval cobblestone alleys dotted with bars, restaurants, hotels, fashion boutiques, old fashioned bread shops, wine shops and fashionable art galleries. The word "Marais" literally means marsh, and until the 12th century, when it was converted to farmland, that's exactly what it was. In 1240 the Order of the Temple built a fortified church in the northern part of the Marais. The Order turned this district into an attractive area, which became known as the Temple Quarter. From that time to the 17th century, and particularly after 1605, when King Henri IV began building the Place Royale (known today as Place des Vosges, the oldest square in Paris), it became a favorite place of residence for the French nobility. They built their spectacular urban mansions there (hotels particuliers), which are some of Paris's best surviving samples of Baroque architecture. During the 17th century though, French nobility started to move to the clearer, less populated and less polluted area of Faubourg Saint- Germain. The district then became a popular and active commercial area, hosting one of Paris' main Jewish communities. By the 1950s, the district had become a working-class area and most of its architectural masterpieces were in a state of ruin. In 1964, the Marais became the first secteur sauvegarde (or safeguarded sector), so that it's cultural significance could be protected and conserved. In the decades that followed, the government and the municipality of Paris have worked together to form an active restoration and Rehabilitation Policy. Nowadays, the Marais has become a fashionable district, home to many trendy restaurants, fashion houses, and galleries.

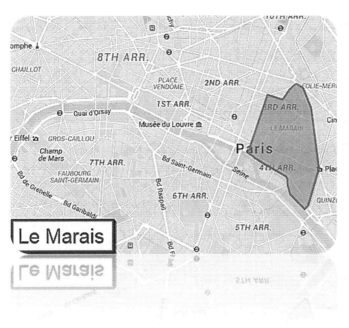

Le Marais

Starting from the Place des Vosges in the east lies the 4th arrondissement part of the Marais. The main Hotels particuliers here have been restored and turned into museums: the Hotel Sale is home to the Picasso Museum, the Hotel Carnavalet is home to the Paris Historical Museum- probably the best place to observe Paris's evolution through the ages. Two of the most beautifully restored Hotel Particuliers are the Hotel Donon, home to the Cognacq-Jay Museum and the magnificent Hotel de Sully with its exquisite garden. Moving on to the western part of Marais, the site of Beaubourg was chosen for the Centre Georges Pompidou, France's national Museum of Modern Art and a world renowned cultural institution. The building was completed in 1977 and is considered a modern masterpiece.

To the north, just a few minutes away from the Pompidou Centre is one of Nicholas Flamel's (the legendary reputed alchemist) houses, at 52 rue de Montmorency. It is the oldest stone house in the city, dating back to 1407 and has been converted into a restaurant. Further north, the quieter 3rd arrondissement part of the Marais is a lovely neighborhood to explore. There you can find the Musee des Arts and Metiers, Europe's oldest science museum.

In the southwestern part of the Marais is the beating heart of the gay community that flourished from the 1980's, spreading out from Rue Vieille du Temple, along Rue St-Croix de la Bretonnerie and finally to Rue du Temple. There you can find trendy cafes, shops, cabarets and nightclubs aimed at gays but welcoming to all.

Montparnasse

Situated on the left bank of the Seine, centered at the crossroads of the Boulevard du Montparnasse and the Rue de Rennes, between the Rue de Rennes and boulevard Raspail is the neighbourhood of Montparnasse. A hill once, the neighborhood took its name from students, who in the 17th century came here to recite poetry. They nicknamed it after "Mount Parnassus", home to the nine Muses of arts and sciences in Greek mythology. Montparnasse was absorbed into the capital's 14th arrondissement in 1669. During the French Revolution many dance halls and cabarets opened their doors. In the 18th century the hill was leveled for the construction of the Boulevard Montparnasse. Much of Montparnasse was leveled in the late 1960s for the construction of the train station and the Tour Montparnasse, Paris's only skyscraper. The Tour Montparnasse has gone under severe criticism for its simple architecture, large proportions and monolithic appearance, as characteristics that are out of place in Paris's urban landscape. As a result, two years after its completion the construction of buildings over seven stories high in the city center was banned. The rooftop terrace though compensates with a spectacular panoramic view of Paris.

Montparnasse became famous in the 1920s and the 1930s as the heart of intellectual and artistic life in Paris. From 1910 to the start of World War II, Paris's artistic circles moved to Montparnasse as an alternative to the Montmartre, which had been the intellectual hub for the previous generation of artists. The cafes and bars of Montparnasse were a meeting place for artists from all over the world. During Montparnasse's prime (from 1910 to 1920), cafes such as Le Dome, La Coupole, La Closerie des Lilas and La Rotonde -note that all of them are still operating— were the places where it was common practice for starving artists to occupy a table all evening for a very small amount of money. While the area attracted people with its creative, bohemian environment, it also became a haven for political exiles such as Vladimir Lenin and Leon Trotsky. But, after the end of World War II the artistic community was dispersed and Montparnasse never regained its former splendor, although it seems to still retain a real-life vibe that some "trendier" parts of Paris seem to have lost.

Another important site of Montparnasse are the Catacombs of Paris, underground ossuaries located at the Place Denfert-Rochereau, where, in their labyrinthine tunnels, centuries worth of Parisians' bones are contained (close to six million people), thus giving it its reputation as "The World's Largest Grave".

Other important sites include the Montparnasse Cemetery, where Charles Baudelaire, Jean-Paul Sartre, Simone de Beauvoir and Samuel Beckett are buried, and the Pasteur Institute, located at Rue du Dr Roux, whose museum houses a collection of memorabilia of Louis Pasteur's life and work, including his funeral chapel.

Opera/Les Grands Boulevards

During the Belle Epoque, the Grands Boulevards were the place in Paris to see, and, most importantly, to be seen, in posh cafes, at the opera, or in the passages couverts (that is, glass-roofed arcades). Today, the Grands Boulevards are the city's shopping epicenter, home to some of the most popular department stores and the Galeries Lafayette and Au Printemps, near Place de l'Opera.

The Grands Boulevards are a major cultural destination, with the magnificent Opera Garnier being their most important stop. "The most famous opera house in the world" (It is the setting for Gaston Leroux's 1910 novel "The Phantom of the Opera"), was commissioned by Napoleon III and built from 1861 to 1875.

The neighborhood is also home to a few exceptional small museums; all former private collections housed in 19th-century private mansions (hotels particuliers). The Musee Jacquemart-Andre is home to an impressive collection of Italian Renaissance art and a magnificent winter garden. Others are the Musee Cernuschi, whose collection of Asian art is second only to the Musee Guimet, and the Musee National Gustave-Moreau, home to a collection of drawings, paintings, watercolors, and sculptures of the Symbolist painter.

The Bastille Area

The Bastille area was the epicenter of the French revolution. The Bastille was built between 1370 and 1383, and initially served as defense to the eastern approach of Paris. It was converted into a prison by Cardinal Richelieu during the 17th century. The place gradually became a place of horror and oppression and a symbol of autocratic cruelty. It was stormed on July 14, 1789 by the people of Paris and subsequently demolished. The Place de la Bastille now stands on its place. The streets around Place de la Bastille are buzzing with people at night due to an array of bars, music clubs, and the Opera Bastille. The large ditch that was behind the fort has been transformed into a marina, called the Basin de l'Arsenal, to the south, bordered by the Boulevard de la Bastille. To the north, the Canal Saint-Martin is brimming with bars, cafes, art galleries, and small designer boutiques. Same goes for Rues Oberkampf, St-Maur, and Jean-Pierre-Timbaud. On Thursdays and

Sundays, a large, open-air market takes place at the park north of the Place de la Bastille, along the Boulevard Richard-Lenoir. Visitors can find everything there, from fresh fruit to clothing and typical flea market items. During excavation for the Metro in 1899, some undemolished remains of the Bastille were found and transferred to a nearby park (the Square Henri-Galli) where they are on display today. The original outline of the Bastille can also be seen marked on the pavement of streets and pathways that pass over its former location.

The Bastille Area

Other noteworthy attractions include the Viaduc des Arts, an urban-renewal project that transformed the railways of the Paris-Bastille - Vincennes train line into arcaded art galleries and shops. Along the top, the Promenade Plantee, a 4.7 km elevated linear park built on top of the obsolete railway infrastructure, makes for a beautiful walk through the 12th arrondissement.

Continuing east lies the city's largest cemetery, Pere-Lachaise, where Honore de Balzac, Frederic Chopin, Eugene Delacroix, Jean de La Fontaine, Amedeo Modigliani, Jim Morrison, Edith Piaf, Marcel Proust and Gertrude Stein are buried among others. To the north is the Parc Buttes-Chaumont, with grassy fields, the Temple de la Sibylle (a miniature version of the famous ancient Roman Temple of Vesta in Tivoli, Italy), and beautiful hilltop views of Paris. It is one of the best places to eat a picnic lunch and rest after a museum-ridden day.

Safety concerns

Paris is generally a safe city, at least as safe as most metropolitan cities can be. In any case it is much safer than most US metropolitan cities. Most probably you will not face any kind of problem during your staying, as long as you use your common sense and follow the advice below.

The most common type of crime in Paris's center, where most tourists move, is pickpocketing. The areas of Champs-Elysees, Notre Dame, and Louvre are a haven for pickpockets, so keep an eye on your personal belongings. Also, you might want to be on alert when you are in the metro and generally at crowded places. Furthermore, it is best to avoid the areas around Les Halles and St-Denis and on Boulevard de Clichy in Pigalle during the night, since illegal trade and hate crimes often take place there. Also avoid Chatelet, Gare du Nord and Stalingrad late at night as well as traveling to the Northern Paris suburbs of Saint-Denis, Aubervilliers, Saint-Ouen and others nearby after dark. It is best to always stay within the 20 arrondisements of central Paris. Women traveling alone, homosexual couples and Jewish people might want to take extra precautions, since it is more probable that they become targets.

Moreover, it is most likely that you will run into one or more of the following scams, so it is best you are aware of them:

- **Sign petition scam:** While walking the streets of Paris various people, mostly women and children might block your path or just approach you and ask you to sign a petition to raise awareness about someone who is suffering, like the hungry children of Africa. The paper will have some signatures to prove its legitimacy. Just ignore them and keep walking, and don't think about signing because it is a scam. After you sign they will find a way to ask you for money. They might tell you that now that you signed you need to give X amount for their cause, or beg you to give whatever you can, or even threaten you that you have signed agreeing that you owe them an X amount of money, e.g. 500 Euros. Even if you signed, just ignore anything that they are telling you and walk away.
- **The ring scam:** While walking in the street, a person, most likely a woman, pretends to have found a golden ring in front of you and asks if it is yours. Even if you say no, she prompts you to take it because it is very valuable, but if you do then she asks for money. The ring of course is

worthless. They mostly act near Champs de Mars, the Eiffel Tower and Jardin des Tuileries. A variation of that is when the scammer drops something near you to make you think you dropped it, and while you try to find out what you dropped they try to steal your wallet.

- **The string around the wrist scam:** A person approaches you with a piece of string or yarn in his hands and offers to make a "friendship bracelet" or "friendship ring" for you. When creating it on your hand, he will tie it so tight that you will not be able to escape. The outcome would be either asking for money to release you, drive you to the nearest ATM to give them money to release you, or keep you occupied with this until his friends scammers steal your wallet or any other valuable possession. This trick is most commonly practiced throughout the Montmartre area and mainly close to the giant staircase that leads to the Sacre Coeur.

- **Other minor scams:** People may approach you and ask if you speak English, or offer flowers if you are a woman. Both will ask for money after that. Be careful in some cafes and restaurants (very few though), they might serve you larger, more expensive drinks than the normal ones, or they might overcharge you so take a look if the bill matches with what you consumed. Don't get distracted when taking money from an ATM or when inside the metro, because some scammers will deliberately try to do that in order to pickpocket you.

Where to stay

Most people that are planning a trip to Paris are concerned with this question. What is the best place to stay in Paris? Is it safe? Is it close to attractions? Is it nice? Are there any stores available nearby for my everyday needs? Does it have access through public transport? It is very reasonable to have those kinds of thoughts when it comes to picking a place for your staying in Paris or any other place in the world. Below you can see a map of the 20 administrative districts "arrondissements" of Paris and the river Seine which divides the city in half.

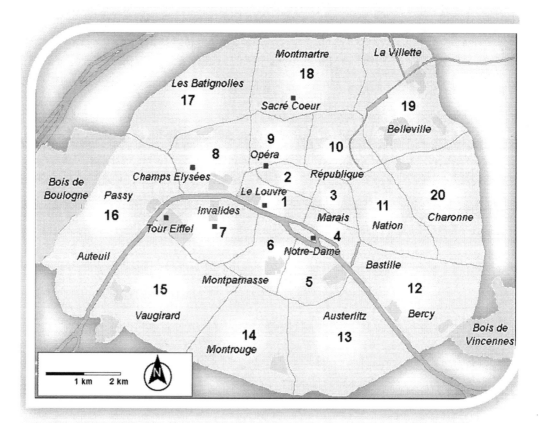

The arrondissements are numbered in a spiral, the center being Ile de la Cite, the island in the Seine, home to Notre-Dame. Arrondissements with lower numbers are closer to the center, while the 12th-20th arrondissements are the outer edge of Paris's center. There is no such thing as the "best neighborhood" to stay in Paris, since it depends on your style, your personality and your expectations from your travel to Paris. Let me describe what each neighborhood has to offer, and then you can decide which one is best for you. In the end I will also give you some general advice on what to avoid when picking the neighborhood that you will stay in Paris.

Tradition has it that the left bank of Seine is the bohemian heart of the city, while the right bank hosts the high-priced sophistication and the world's best shopping. The truth is that Paris's center is a mix of the above in both banks of the river.

Saint-Germain-des-Pres (6th arrondissement)

St. Germain is fashionable and chic. It has trendy bars, nightclubs, restaurants, little shops and art galleries. Some of the city's best known cafes are situated here, and the smaller streets between this busy thoroughfare and the river harbor have some truly exceptional small restaurants and other specialty shops. The gorgeous Luxembourg Gardens are an easy walk in this district of Paris. The very picturesque church of Saint-Germain-des-Pres, built over uneven cobblestone and offering a kind of fortress-like feeling, towers over the square. Also nearby is Saint Sulpice and its lovely square (one of France's most famous actresses lives here). If you're going to stay in the north part, Ile de la Cite will be very close. You'll likely pay a bit of a premium for staying in this part of town, but there are some bargains to be found as you move away from the river.

Le Marais (3rd / 4th arrondissement)

The Marais is in a central location. It's got several attractions nearby, like the Centre Pompidou and the Hotel de Ville (Paris City Hall). There are lots of restaurants and cafes, plus the architecture is magnificent. Locals head to the Marais for nighttime entertainment. The Marais was once a largely Jewish neighborhood, and in fact there is still a significant and active Jewish population here. Also, the Marais is one of the best shopping neighborhoods in the city with many independently owned boutiques as well as luxury shops and wonderful markets. Since a great many of the shops here are open on Sunday, Sunday afternoon strolls through the Marais are a must. If you move north a little bit in the Marais, especially towards the part of the 3rd arrondissement, you'll find things significantly quieter.

Opera (2nd / 9th)

The area around the Opera is not a very touristy place because it doesn't have as many attractions as other parts of Paris. Nonetheless it's very Parisian, situated in the heart of Paris, and a great base for exploring it. It is mostly a residential zone, but with tons of restaurants, bars and cafes, especially on Boulevard Haussmann. The Opera, Galeries Lafayette, plus some small private museums are situated here. The Louvre and the banks of river Seine are merely a 10 minute walk, plus you won't have to deal with the hordes of tourists like other parts of central Paris.

Latin Quarter (5th)

The Latin Quarter is one of the most centrally located neighborhoods of Paris, and it's a relatively easy walk to the majority of attractions from there. Younger people tend to fill the streets, something that makes the area known for its nightlife. Most establishments here are open till late, and people stay out in cafes and bars until the early hours of the morning. This wild nightlife party is located mostly at the intersection of Saint Michel and Saint Germain Blvds and radiating out toward the Seine to both east and west. Of course there are calmer neighborhoods as well, such as those surrounding the Pantheon and those further south and east, in the area around rue des Ecoles and the smaller streets in the vicinity of rue Saint Jacques. Thus one can be centrally located without having to give up a good night's sleep. The Latin Quarter offers inexpensive to moderately priced places to stay.

At the Latin Quarter you will find a rich variety of restaurants, mostly inexpensive to moderately priced, representing virtually any ethnicity you can think of. Also, there are a lot of cafes and bars for all tastes. Shopping is also focused on the youth, but you will also find a large number of specialty stores and unusual little boutiques dating back to the eleventh century. Many lovely bookstores, both general as well as highly specialized, conclude this amazing scenery.

Monmarte (18th)

Montmartre is a village-like urban neighborhood, also depicted in the film "Amelie". Montmartre was long the bohemian Mecca of Paris's art and music set. Even today, street artists in Place du Tertre at the top of the hill will approach you to draw a painting of you or your companions. The surrounding area of Place du Tertre is gorgeous and has a magnificent view of the city, plus there is a street youth party on the stairs of Sacre-Coeur almost every day! Tiny winding streets snake around stone walls with quiet restaurants and cafes on the hillside. You're a little off the beaten path up in Monmarte, which is one very good reason to stay here. Of course metro and bus lines can take you anywhere you want to go in your everyday little Paris trips. Staying in Monmarte is a little risky though, since not all parts are very safe. Rue Lepic and its side streets are lovely, while the Pigalle area and further east are not so safe, so you'd better avoid staying there. The best way to know if you're in the good part of Montmartre is the Google Street View! Take a look at the neighborhood before you book an accommodation, in order to be sure that the neighborhood is ok.

Ile Saint-Louis (4th)

The Ile Saint-Louis is the smaller of the two islands in the Seine and since it has no government offices on it, it's calm and relatively quiet. Ile Saint-Louis is situated in the dead center of Paris. As mentioned before, Notre-Dame Cathedral, located in Ile de la Cite, which is pretty close, is point zero of Paris. It feels like Ile Saint-Louis is a small town, separated from Paris even though it's next door to Ile de la Cite and the massive crowds of tourists visiting Notre-Dame. The shops are pretty good, and the scenery is quite picturesque. You can find some great restaurants and some exotic or even bizarre shops here. There aren't many places to stay, and they are quite expensive, but the charm and hospitality are unbeatable. Since this is the very center of the city, most of the buildings date back at least as far as the eighteenth century, and many well before that, something that makes the accommodations here really interesting.

Eiffel tower (7th), Champs Elysees (8th) and the Louvre (1st)

First-time visitors often want to be near the Eiffel Tower or the Champs Elysees, so they mostly search for accommodation near those places. The area around the Eiffel Tower is nice and clean, but there are very few interesting shops and restaurants in the area. Sometimes it feels deserted, since most people come here to visit the Eiffel Tower, and then go to more interesting neighborhoods. Trocadero though is a place that many people hang out, since it offers an amazing view of the Eiffel Tower night and day, and you can enjoy a glass of wine in one of the lovely bars and restaurants behind the square, or just take some pictures from the Jardins du Trocadero. If you only have time to visit the Eiffel Tower or you want to admire it from your balcony, then this might be a good location for you. If not, it is best to stay in one of the aforementioned neighborhoods.

The area around Champs-Elysees and near the Arc de Triomphe tends to be overpriced and touristy, so it is best to avoid staying here as well. If you do want to stay in a luxury hotel, you might want to look at Place Vendome (1st arrondissement), where some of the most luxurious hotels and shops of Paris are located. Place Vendome is also close to Place de la Concorde, Palais Royal, the Louvre Museum and the Tuileries.

Where not to stay

Since we have mentioned what each neighborhood has to offer, you can now decide which one is best for you. I will only sum up what to avoid and add one or two more to what I have already mentioned:

- It is best not to stay outside the main 20 arrondissements, since you will be far from the center and while many of Paris's surrounding suburbs are lovely and safe, some of them are the most dangerous areas in Paris. Not to mention that public transport will be more expensive if you travel from to zone 1 (the 20 arrondissements) from other zones (suburbs), so even if you are travelling on a budget, staying outside the 20 arrondissements might not be as cheap as you may think.
- Don't stay in a hotel near the airport. Unless it's for one night only and your flight leaves at 6:00 a.m. the next day. Paris's two airports, Charles de Gaulle and Orly, are both far outside the city.
- Don't plan your stay around being close to a certain attraction. Paris's metro is easy and efficient enough to navigate your way anywhere — you don't need to stay within walking distance from the Louvre in order to visit the Louvre.
- "Near the Eiffel Tower" actually isn't that great. The neighborhoods near the Eiffel Tower are upscale residential areas. They're fine, but they're expensive and a bit boring, in my opinion. Besides, you can see the tower from all over the city.
- "Near the Champs-Elysees" is worse. Definitely go to the Champs-Elysees at least once, but it's filled with shops you can find anywhere and it's absolutely swarming with tourists. It's Paris's "Times Square".

What to eat

France is famous worldwide for its cuisine, so when you are going to Paris you need to make sure you taste at least some specific delicacies. Paris is full of restaurants and street food vendors, and a first time visitor is usually confused on what to choose. This guide is not meant to advertise specific businesses, and my advice is you download a mobile application with user's reviews for restaurants and then decide in which you eat. The "useful apps" section of this guide will help you with that. Back to French cuisine now and what is has to offer to your palette:

Breakfast

The French breakfast or "le petit dejeuner" is really small, and usually consisted of croissant and coffee. The name "croissant" means "crescent" and refers to the shape of the pastry. The Parisians might eat mostly croissants for breakfast, but they have so many of them. Pastries in Paris are an art form and they are light, flaky and crisp on the outside, and chewy on the inside. Paris is full of "Patisseries" ready to offer a wide variety of pastries, filled with whatever your mind might think of. Besides the traditional croissant, other popular pastry options include:

- **Pain au Raisin** – A pastry with a sweet custard-like filling and raisins, usually rolled in a spiral.
- **Pain au Chocolat** – A pastry with a filling of pieces of chocolate.
- **Chausson aux Pommes** – A pastry folded in half and baked with a filling akin to apple sauce.

There are other pastries in Paris as well like eclairs and profiteroles – but they are mostly eaten as desserts.

Also you can always enjoy the famous French bread, the traditional baguette, with some butter and jam as an alternative for breakfast. Brioche is another choice. Brioches have a touch of sweetness, but not nearly as much as the pastries listed above.

Lunch or Dinner

In many Parisian restaurants, lunch (le dejeuner) and dinner (le diner) menus are either the same, slightly different, or lunch is a smaller version of dinner. A typical French lunch or dinner is consisted of:

1. A starter (entree), such as soup, a mixed salad, some terrine or pate.
2. A main course (le plat principal), mostly a choice of meat or fish, with rice, potatoes, pasta and vegetables.
3. A cheese course or a dessert course. Common choices for desserts include fruit tarts, creme brulee, creme caramel or ice-cream. Cheese courses include a mix of various types of French cheese. Coffee at the end of the meal is an optional extra.

Most restaurants offer fixed price menus with two or three courses, with the ability to choose from a selection of plates. So, a three course meal, might offer you a choice between 2-3 of each entry plates, main plates and desserts. In French you will see them as "Entree + Plat + dessert". Almost all restaurants also offer free choice of things to eat (eating a la carte). Menu prices for 3 courses can start from about 20€ per person. You can have a great meal in a descent restaurant for 25-30€ per person, but depending on the restaurant you might enjoy good cuisine with as low as 20€ per person as well.

Some of the dishes you might want to try are:

- **Escargots** – Snails served with the little critters still in their shells, cooked in a sumptuous buttery sauce.
- **Steak Tartare** – A finely chopped raw beef that's been marinated and seasoned. It is cooked through being marinated in alcohol, but it's still mostly raw.
- **Onion Soup** – A rich beef-based broth full of onions, cooked until they're soft and sweet, and then covered with cheese and baked in the oven.

- **Croque Monsieur/Madame** – A croque **monsieur** is a grilled sandwich with cheese on the outside and ham on the inside. The "**madame**" adds a sunny-side-up egg to the top.
- **Boeuf Bourguignon** – A slow-cooked beef stew with a substantial quantity of Burgundy wine poured into the sauce. Mostly eaten during the winter.
- **Moules** – When they are in season, there are signs for moules (mussels) in front of almost every restaurant in Paris. They are a Parisian must-have, and worth trying. You might also want to try "mouclade" instead, which is actually just a variation of mussels baked in a cream and white wine sauce.
- **Confit de Canard** – This is duck confit, and if you have never tried duck, it is the best time to do so in Paris. A Confit de Canard is flavorful, tender, and could serve as a stand-in for just about any comfort food you can imagine.
- **Coq au Vin** – This is a chicken dish cooked in wine and it is mostly a winter dish.

As I said you don't need to give your right arm to enjoy those specialties. I remember one time I enjoyed a great 3 course meal of **Onion Soup - Confit de Canard – Creme brulee** for as little as 22€ per person plus some extraordinary bulk red wine.

Street Food

Street food in Paris is wonderful, and is one of the things you must try. It's quick, it's cheap, it can fill your belly in no time when between your daily attraction tours and it's also an experience, like trying all the other types of food mentioned above. It is not difficult to find street food in Paris, you will find it available in every corner. One thing is for sure; you won't get hungry in Paris! There are 4 main types of street food:

- **Falafel** – A fried dough made from ground chickpeas and formed into golf ball sized balls. Most often it is served in a pita and dressed with condiments.
- **Crepes** – Ultra-thin pancakes filled with just about anything you could imagine and then folded up. Can be sweet, for example filled with chocolate, or savory.
- **Sandwiches**–There are sandwiches filled with anything you can imagine from pork and chicken, to tuna and vegetables; most of them also have some

kind of cheese in them. If you want you can requested it toasted with no extra charge.

- **Galettes** – Ultra-thin pancakes served with fillings and folded up. Galettes are mostly made from buckwheat flour, and are mainly savory.

Dessert

Desserts are almost always included in a French menu. Below are some incredible desserts that you must try while being in Paris:

Clafoutis – A sponge cake that is baked with whatever fruits are in season.

Creme brulee– This is a dessert consisting of a rich custard base topped with a contrasting layer of hard caramel. It is normally served at room temperature and the custard is usually flavored with vanilla.

Iles Flottantes – "Iles Flottantes" or "floating islands," is a dessert consisted of small quantities of meringue floating in a pool of creme anglaise, a vanilla-cream sauce.

Macarons – Macarons are light cookies made from egg whites and almond flour that sandwich a layer of cream in various flavors, or chocolate, or jam. They are multi-colored, soft and very tasty.

Madeleines – Madeleines are very small sponge cakes with a distinctive shell-like shape, which is acquired from being baked in pans with shell-shaped depressions.

Those are some of the desserts that are prominent in the French cuisine, but of course tasting other desserts like ice-cream, hot chocolate or profiteroles will be an unforgettable experience as well. For those who do not have a sweet tooth though, there is always the option of ordering a plate of various types of cheese.

Transportation

Paris has an excellent public transport system, which will allow you to move wherever you want easily and inexpensively. There is a variety of public transport means that you can use. Others are practical and cheap and others more expensive but nicer, even romantic, so let's see your alternatives.

Metro

The metro is the ideal way to get around Paris, because it is fast, easy and inexpensive. The Paris metro system has 16 lines traversing the city and each line has a different color and number. Despite the large number of different lines, the Paris metro is very easy to use, and you will understand that once you look at the metro map. At any given Metro station each Metro line has 2 platforms, one for each direction, as in most metros worldwide. Each direction is marked by its terminus station, the last station on the line.

You will find a Metro map on the wall while descending into a Metro station and also on the platform wall. What you need to do is find the station you are at, and then find the station you want to travel to. Once you find your destination station on the map, just mentally follow the Metro line to its end, the terminus, which will be the direction name you need for this Metro line.

Tickets

Metro tickets (or "t+") start at 1.80 Euros per ticket, but if you are planning to use the metro for your transportation, you might want to buy a "carnet" of 10 tickets and get approximately 20% discount. Each ticket is valid for one trip including changes within the metro system. What's cool is that you can use the same tickets in other public transportation means as well (like the bus)! Also, you have the choice to buy a pass for 1, 2, 3 and 5 days, and a pass for 1 month. If you are going to enter and exit the metro many times during a day, you might want to consider buying a pass for the days you are going to need it for.

A key thing you must know is that Paris metropolitan area is divided in 5 zones and not all tickets are valid for all of them, so you must check before you buy. CDG airport is in zone 5, Orly and Versailles in Zone 4 and the city of Paris is Zone 1. That means that after going to the city center once you arrive in Paris, you will mainly move within zone 1 which is the 20 arrondisments including almost all well-known Paris attractions, thus you don't need to buy tickets that apply to zones outside zone 1 since they will be more expensive.

The validity range of a single ticket depends on the transportation that you are using. So, on the metro, a single ticket is valid for one trip to any metro station regardless of its zone location, while on the RER (see below) a single metro ticket is valid only inside Zone 1 (within Paris). On the buses and trams a single metro ticket is valid for 90 minutes in any single direction, with interchanges to other buses/trams included. In certain bus lines higher priced tickets are required, depending on the length of the trip. These are the Orlybus, Noctilien, Balabus, Roissybus, and lines 299, 350 and 351. You can buy tickets, even carnets, from automatic ticket machines located in almost every metro station in Paris.

Buses

Buses are another alternative option of Paris's public transportation. Moving using buses will allow you to see and enjoy the city, but since Paris has a lot of traffic, it will slow you down, something that is not good if you are in a tight schedule trying to see as many attractions as possible. As mentioned above, tickets for buses are the same as the ones you use in the metro. A "t+" ticket (metro ticket) allows transfers among buses for up to 90 minutes from the first trip. Note that there can be no transfers between bus and metro lines. Lastly, keep in mind that the metro stops between 12.30 and 1 a.m., and buses stop between 9 and 10 p.m., with reduced service continuing with night buses and Noctilien buses. Using the metro during the day, and night buses and Noctilien during the night when the metro stops is the easiest and cheapest choice you have. Again, note that night buses and Noctilien are more expensive and more than one ticket might be required for a certain route.

Boats

A real fun and romantic way to get around Paris is the boat. The Batobus is a bus line with 9 stops along the Seine. Batobus stops at every known monument in the city: Beaugrenelle at Port de Javel Haut, Tour Eiffel (port de Boudonnais), Musee d'Orsay (Port de Solferino), Saint-Germain-des-pres (Port Malaquais), Notre Dame (Port Montebello), Jardin des Plantes (Port saint Bernard), Hotel de Ville (Port de l' Hotel de Ville), Louvre (Port de Louvre) and Champs-Elysees (port des Champs-Elysees). Batobus is a bit more expensive though, at 16 Euros per day for an adult and of course its stops are only suitable for visiting specific attractions located across the Seine. So, I would suggest you use Batobus only for the experience of using it, and only for 1 day, since moving to other parts of Paris's center is not possible.

Hop On/Hop off buses

Like many other cities, Paris has a Hop on/Hop off line of buses that cover the main tourist attractions. They have 50 stops in Paris, with four circuits on one ticket, and you can get on and off as many times as you want. If you are short in time and want to have a quick view of the main attractions with an occasional stop, you can use them. Like anywhere else though, Hop on/Hop off buses are an expensive way to see the city, and more specifically in Paris start from 30€ per adult per day.

RER

The RER in Paris is an integration of a modern city-center underground rail and a pre-existing set of commuter rail lines. The RER is a good way to get from one point to another very fast since it has fewer stops. The lines are fewer though as well. You will mainly need the RER if you want to travel to nearby suburbs. Tickets within zone 1 are the same as metro tickets, but outside zone 1, a billet Ile-de-France rather than a normal Ticket t is required.

If you need to go to suburbs located even further to where RER goes, you need to use SNCF commuter trains.

Trains

Paris has a very organized train system with six train stations. The stations are:

1. Gare Saint Lazare
2. Gare du Nord
3. Gare de l'Est
4. Gare de Lyon
5. Gare d'Austerlitz
6. Gare Montparnasse

Each of them serve a different part of France, and some of them even serve other countries. There are RER and/or metro services to access all of them.

Paris's main attractions

The Louvre

The Louvre is one of the world's largest museums hosting some of the greatest works of all times. It hosts almost 35,000 pieces dating from pre – history to the 21st century in an area of more than 650,000 square feet (60,000 square meters). It is the most visited museum in the world with more than 9 million visitors per year!

The building itself was originally built as a fortress in the 12th century. It was extended many times, and finally was transformed to a palace, the Louvre Palace. The museum first opened in 1793 with only 537 paintings. Today the collection is divided among eight curatorial departments: Egyptian Antiquities; Near Eastern Antiquities; Greek, Etruscan, and Roman Antiquities; Islamic Art; Sculpture; Decorative Arts; Paintings; Prints and Drawings.

The Louvre museum is divided into three "wings":

• The Sully Wing is the East wing, and it was named after Maximilien de Bethune, the first Duke of Sully (1560–1641), who was the Finance Minister and chief advisor to King Henry IV.

• The Richelieu Wing is the north wing and runs for several blocks along the Rue de Rivoli. It is named after Cardinal Richelieu (Armand Jean du Plessis, 1585–1642), who was not only a Cardinal but also the Chief Minister of King Louis XIII, the son of Henry IV.

• The Denon Wing is the south wing and it stretches along the right bank of the Seine. It is named after Dominique Vivant, Baron Denon (1747–1825), an archeologist, diplomat, author and artist, who was appointed by Napoleon as the first director of the Louvre Museum in 1802. In the Denon Wing you will find the Mona Lisa, the Crowning of Napoleon and other well-known works. That is why it is the most crowded wing of all three.

Louvre Museum opening hours are:

• Monday, Thursday, Saturday, and Sunday: from 9 a.m. to 6 p.m.

• Wednesday, Friday: from 9 a.m. to 9:45 p.m.

• Closed on Tuesdays

• Rooms begin closing 30 minutes before museum closing time.

The museum has three entrances:

• Pyramid and Galerie du Carrousel entrances: open every day (except Tuesday) from 9 a.m. to 7:30 p.m. on Mondays, Thursdays, Saturdays, and Sundays; and from 9 a.m. to 10 p.m. on Wednesdays and Fridays.

• Passage Richelieu entrance: open every day (except Tuesday) from 9 a.m. to 5:30 p.m. (6:30 p.m. on Wednesdays and Fridays)

• Porte des Lions entrance: open every day except Tuesday and Friday. Opening hours are not standard in this gate so you need to call at +33 (0) 1 40 20 53 17 to ask.

You can buy tickets for Louvre online at http://www.louvre.fr/en

If you decide to buy tickets after getting there, keep in mind that the museum ticket offices accept payments only in cash (Euros only) or by card (credit or debit). Bank cards can be used on the automatic distributors as well. Filming and photography are permitted in the permanent collection exhibition rooms, but the use of flash and other lighting equipment is not permitted. Filming and photography though, are not allowed in the temporary exhibition rooms.

Website: http://www.louvre.fr/en

Tel: +33 (0)1 40 20 53 17 (except Tuesdays)

Address: 75001 Paris, France

Coordinates: 48.8611° N, 2.3364° E

The Eiffel Tower

The Eiffel Tower stands on the south bank of the Seine in a garden known as the Champ de Mars, between the Seine and the Ecole Militaire. The Eiffel Tower was built in 1889 and for 41 years, until 1930, it was the world's tallest man-made structure, with 1,063 feet (324 meters) height. It also holds various other records as well, including being the most visited paid-entrance tourist attraction in the world, but also it is one of the most recognized structures in the world.

The Eiffel tower was designed by Gustave Eiffel, one of France's greatest 19th century engineers. It was designed as a gateway to the Paris Universal Exhibition, marking the centenary of the French Revolution of 1789. It was originally put up on a 20-year lease, with a plan to be dismantled in 1909, but by then it had become such a popular landmark that Paris city Hall decided to keep it open. It is built from 7,300 tons of iron. Skeptics thought that the tower will not be stable, and might even blow over by fierce wind, but Eiffel proved them wrong, since his design was so successful that even in the strongest wind the top of the tower only moves by about 7 centimeters.

The Tower has three levels, and there are restaurants and coffee houses on the first and the second level. Most visitors use the elevators to the first and second levels, but many use the stairs, in order to enjoy the view plus not wait up the 3 or 4 hour queues for the lifts! Access to the top (third level) is by elevator only.

The Eiffel Tower can be seen from all over Paris, and most notably from the heights of Montmartre or from the top of Notre Dame. The best place to view it from a distance is just across the Seine, from the Esplanade of the Trocadero, right opposite. You will see crowds of people capturing amazing photographs and videos of the Eiffel Tower from there. There are public toilets on the first and second levels, but not at the top level.

It is best to buy your ticket online before going to Paris, in order to avoid endless queues, especially during spring and summer months until early October. You can buy tickets online from the Tower's official website at http://ticket.toureiffel.fr/

Website (New): http://www.toureiffel.paris/

Tel: +33 (0)8 92 700 016

Address: Champ de Mars, 5 Avenue Anatole France, 75007 Paris, France

Coordinates: 48.8582° N, 2.2945° E

Cathedrale Notre-Dame de Paris

Notre-Dame de Paris (French for "Our Lady of Paris") is a great example of Gothic architecture, actually one of the first Gothic Cathedrals in Europe, and one of the most recognized Cathedrals worldwide. Movies and animations were filmed here or had Notre Dame as their central theme. It is the home of Quasimodo, the church where Napoleon was crowned and many French kings were married. It is the symbolic heart of France and ground zero of Paris, which means all distances to and from the city are measured from this spot. Its construction begun in 1163 and lasted for 182 years until 1345, the year it was completed. It sustained serious damage during the French revolution, but it was fully restored to its former glory in 1845, and further maintenance was done in 1991.

Notre Dame is an amazing example of gothic architecture with many gargoyles watching it night and day. If you don't have a problem with heights, you can go to the top and enjoy one of the most beautiful views of Paris. On the left of the church there is a separate entrance which leads to the 387 steps of the south tower, which is accessible to public. At the end of those steps you will find its magnificent bell. From up there you can see Monmarte on the north, the Arc de Triomphe to the west, and the Pantheon to the south. Usually there is a large queue at the steps, except weekdays' mornings, where things are a bit better.

In front of Notre Dame there is an archaeological museum called "Crypte Archeologique". It goes back to when Paris was a Roman city called Lutetia, and offers a subterranean view of the area from the 1st century through medieval times. A renovation that took place in 2012 cleaned up the remains of this crypt and added 3D video touch-screen panels that bring the ruins to life.

The best time to visit Notre Dame is early in the morning, when the cathedral is at its brightest and has less visitors. English audio-guides are available at the entrance for a small fee. Also, free guided tours in English are offered 2 –3 times each week, which you can verify by calling and asking for information. Entrance to the Cathedral is for free, as it is in all Cathedrals and churches in France.

Website: http://www.notredamedeparis.fr/

Tel: +33 (0)1 42 34 56 10

Address: 6 Parvis Notre-Dame - Pl. Jean-Paul II, 75004 Paris, France

Coordinates: 48.8530° N, 2.3498° E

Arc de Triomphe

The Arc de Triomphe is one of the most famous monuments in Paris. It was built by Napoleon after his victory at Austerlitz, but was not finished until 1836, 15 years after Napoleon's death in exile. It was inspired by Rome's Arch of Titus, since Napoleon liked to consider himself the heir to Roman emperors. Around the top of the Arch there are engravings with the names of the major victories won during the Revolutionary and Napoleonic wars. On the walls inside, you will see the names of other victories as well as those of great generals. Beneath the Arch is the Tomb of the Unknown Soldier and the eternal flame commemorating the dead from the devastating first and second World Wars.

Positioned at the intersection of 12 Avenues, at the end of the Champs Elysees, Arc de Triomphe stands 165 feet (49.5 meters) in height, 148 feet (45 meters) wide and

72 feet (22 meters) deep. It is the second largest triumphal arch in the world, with only the Roman Arch of Titus being bigger. There is a lift that takes visitors to the top, where there is a small museum containing large models of the Arc and information on its history from the time of its construction. Also, you can go to the top of the Arch after climbing 46 stairs, and you will see the star effect of the 12 radiating avenues, plus you get an amazing view of Champs-Elysees.

The traffic circle around the Arc is named after Charles de Gaulle, but it is widely known to Parisians as "L' Etoile" or "the Star". Be wary of the traffic circle that surrounds the arch since many accidents have happened here during past years. Don't try to cross the circle above the ground since there is a safe underground passage from the northeast corner of the Avenue des Champs-Elysees which will take you to the Arch.

Website: http://www.arcdetriompheparis.com/

Tel: +33 1 55 37 73 77

Address: Place Charles de Gaulle, 75008 Paris, France

Coordinates: 48.8738° N, 2.2950° E

Basilique du Sacre Coeur

Sacre Coeur or "The Basilica of the Sacred Heart of Paris" is a Roman Catholic Church dedicated to the sacred heart of Jesus. It was designed by Paul Abadie, and its construction began in 1875, its purpose being to symbolize the return of self-confidence after the devastating years of the Paris Commune and Franco-Prussian War, and was finished in 1914. It was consecrated in 1919.

Sacre Coeur is located on the highest point of the city, at the top of Monmarte hill. Many people go to admire the fabulous view from its 271 foot high dome (82 meters), but even the views from the stairs or even below the stairs of the church are amazing, compensating for your effort to climb up there.

The interior decoration of Sacre Coeur is also fabulous. The golden mosaic above the choir, "Christ in Majesty" which was created by Luc-Olivier Merson in 1922 and depicts Christ with a golden heart and outstretched arms with Virgin Mary and Joan of Arc accompanying Him will stun you. Another amazing thing you will see in Sacre Coeur is its huge and magestic pipe organ built by Aristide Cavaille-Coll. The organ was originally built for a private home in Biarritz and is composed of 109 ranks and 78 speaking stops that spread across four 61-note manuals and the 32-note pedalboard. It would be a great experience to hear this extraordinary organ live. Also, Sacre Coeur has one of the world's heaviest bells, weighing about 19 tons, and 262 feet (80 meters) tall.

The basilica also has an impressive crypt with entrance at the left side of the basilica (on the outside). Down there you will find the tombs of Cardinals Guibert and Richard, an urn containing the heart of Alexandre Legentil, the initiator of the National Vow, the foundation stone of the Basilica and many more interesting things.

The best time to visit Sacre Coeur is early in the morning or early in the evening, and it would be very interesting to watch a mass there. If you don't want to climb the stairs, there is a furnicular available, and it will spare you a lot of time and effort, for one metro ticket each way. The entrance to Sacre Coeur is free, but if you plan to visit the Dome or the Crypt you must pay an entrance fee.

Website: http://www.sacre-coeur-montmartre.com/

Tel: +33 1 53 41 89 00

Address: 35 Rue du Chevalier de la Barre, 75018 Paris, France

Coordinates: 48.8867° N, 2.3430° E

Les Invalides

Hotel des Invalides is a large complex of 17th century structures built by Louis XIV as a combination of hospital and living quarters for injured or retired military personnel. At the end of the 17th century 4,000 military men lived here, and even today a part of it is used as residence and hospital for veterans. It also has two impressive churches: Eglise du Dome and Eglise St-Louis des Invalides.

The Invalides is the eternal home of Napoleon Bonaparte (1769–1821), since his tomb was moved here in 1840 from the island of Saint Helena, where he died in 1821 in forced exile, after King Louis Philippe I was granted approval from the British to have the remains exhumed and returned to France. Upon being returned to French soil, Napoleon I was given a glorious funeral and placed in a side chapel of the church until a more appropriate crypt could be constructed. The excavation and decoration of the circular well took another 20 years, and today it stands directly under the gold-plated dome where his coffins (Napoleon's body is protected by a series of six coffins one set inside the next, sort of like a Russian nesting doll) lie encased in a massive sarcophagus of red Russian porphyry. Around the tomb you will see a dozen winged figures symbolizing his military achievements. There are many great men accompanying Napoleon is his last residence including his son, Napoleon II, his two brothers, Joseph and Jerome, as well as WWI Marshall

Ferdinand Foch, Claude Joseph Rouget de Lisle - composer of the French national anthem - and many others.

A must visit is the "Musee de l'Armee", the Army Museum, which contains an extensive collection of military artifacts from antique armors and weapons to more modern ones. Medieval weapons and armor including representations of knights in 1:1 scale, elaborate and eccentric 17th to 19th century guns, WWI and WWII exhibits and many more await you to admire them in this amazing museum.

Also, the gardens in front of the Hotel des Invalides, are a known spot for soccer, Frisbee games, dog walking and sunbathing, especially during the summer, despite signs asking people to stay off the grass!

Website: http://www.musee-armee.fr/en/english-version.html

Tel: +33 810 11 33 99

Address: 129 Rue de Grenelle, 75007 Paris, France

Coordinates: 48.8550° N, 2.3125° E

Pantheon

The Pantheon was originally built as a church dedicated to St. Genevieve, the patron saint of Paris, and to house the reliquary chasse containing her relics. After many changes though, it operates today as a secular mausoleum containing the remains of distinguished French citizens. It is an example of neoclassicism, its exterior built like the Pantheon of Rome, surmounted by a dome that used San Pietro in Montorio church in Rome as a model.

Its construction begun on September 6, 1764 and completed in 1790, after King Louis XV vowed in 1744 to erect a church dedicated to Saint Genevieve if he survived his serious illness.

In the entrance you can see the inscription "AUX GRANDS HOMMES LA PATRIE RECONNAISSANTE", which means "To great men, the grateful homeland". By burying its great people in the Pantheon, the French Nation acknowledges the honor it received from them, and as such, interment here is severely restricted and is allowed only by a parliamentary act for "National Heroes". So, here you can admire the graves of great men like Voltaire, the famous French enlightenment writer, Rousseau, the well-known political philosopher, Victor Hugo, writer of "Les Miserables" and "Notre-Dame de Paris", Emile Zola, widely known for the Dreyfus affair, Alexander Dumas, the writer of "the Three Musketeers", Jean Moulin, Louis Braille and many more.

Website: http://www.pantheonparis.com/

Tel: +33 1 44 32 18 00

Address: Place du Pantheon, 75005 Paris, France

Coordinates: 48.8461° N, 2.3458° E

Palace of Versailles

The Palace of Versailles is located at Versailles, about 20 kilometers southwest of Paris. The court of Versailles was the center of political power in France from 1682 until 1789, when the royal family forcibly returned to Paris after the start of the French Revolution. Today the sheer size of the chateau is awe inspiring, but when Louis XIV came here from Paris in 1682 with nearly 20,000 courtiers, noblemen and all sorts of servants following him it didn't seem large enough. The enormous Baroque chateau originally began in 1623 as a hunting lodge, made out of brick and stone, for Louis XIII. It was his successor, Louis XIV, who expanded it as a royal palace. There were two main phases of expansion and a number of remodelations and additions until Louis XVI became King, after which only a few changes to the main palace were made. Near the palace are other, subsidiary structures, of which the two most famous are the Petit Trianon, originally built for Louis XV's mistress Madame de Pompadour and later given to Marie Antoinette by Louis XVI, and the Hameau, a rustic retreat built for Marie Antoinette where she could indulge in the joys of a more domesticated life.

The most celebrated room of the palace is the Galerie des Glaces (Hall of Mirrors), where lavish balls were once part of the daily agenda. The room is also famous for another reason; it was the place where the Treaty of Versailles was signed on 28 June 1919, marking the end of World War I. The Grands Appartements (State Apartments) respectively known as the grand appartement du roi (King) and the grand appartement de la reine (Queen), occupied the main or principal floor of the palace in a "U" shape, with majestically painted ceilings, marble walls, parquet floors, and sumptuous decoration. The Chambre de la Reine (Queen's Bed Chamber) is probably the most opulent bedroom in the world, initially made for Marie Therese, first and only official wife of Louis XIV, and lastly occupied by Marie-Antoinette. The Petits Appartements (Private Apartments) is where the royal family and friends lived. The restored state of the rooms that visitors can see today closely replicate the petit appartement de la reine as it appeared during Marie-Antoinette's day. The sumptuously painted ceilings, tapestries and even the furniture have been returned to their original state. Of all the features of the petit appartement de la reine, the most legendary is the so-called "secret passage" that links the grand appartement de la reine with the appartement du roi. Dating from the time of Marie-Therese, it served as a private means of communication between the king and the queen. Marie Antoinette used it to escape from the Paris mob on the night of 5/6 October 1789.

The Royal Opera, the first oval hall in France, was commissioned by Louis XV and inaugurated in 1770 for the marriage of the dauphin, later Louis XVI, to Marie-Antoinette. It is considered the finest 18th-century opera house in Europe, with excellent acoustics, as a result of being entirely built of wood. Notice that it is painted in faux marble to represent stone.

The white-and-gold chapel, completed in 1710, is where the king and queen attended daily Mass seated in gilt boxes.

Despite its significant size, the palace of Versailles can get extremely crowded, especially as visitors are channeled through one narrow side in the majority of the rooms, with the furniture and other objects roped off. There are also considerable lines, so it is best to arrive here as early as 9 a.m. to avoid them. The main entrance is near the top of the courtyard to the right. There are audio guides available, and also frequent guided tours in English that go through the private royal apartments. Hour-long tours are also available, where you can explore the opera house or Marie-Antoinette's private parlors. The grandest rooms, such as the Hall of Mirrors and Marie-Antoinette's impressive bedchamber can be visited without a group tour. There are brochures at the information office or ticket counter to help the visitor. Also, check the official site of the chateau for admission fees and opening hours.

Website: http://en.chateauversailles.fr/homepage

Tel: +33 01 30 83 78 00

Address: Versailles, France, Coordinates: 48.804404°N 2.123162°E

Free Attractions

Paris has the reputation of being one of the most expensive cities in the world. Nonetheless, that doesn't mean you have to spend a fortune to see Paris's beautiful attractions. There are many attractions, including cathedrals, museums, parks, fashion shows etc. that you can enjoy for free. In this chapter I will present to you the best free attractions you can visit during your stay in Paris.

Cathedrale Notre-Dame de Paris

As we saw in the previous chapter "Paris main attractions", Notre Dame is one of the most popular attractions in Paris. It is a dominating figure on the Ile de la Cite, in the middle of the Seine. It is essential for every visitor to admire its exterior of gargoyles and Gothic touches but also the magnificent stained glass windows in the interior.

Notre Dame is free to visit, as all the churches in France are, although some parts of them, such as towers or crypts, usually have an entrance fee.

Website: http://www.notredamedeparis.fr/

Tel: +33 (0)1 42 34 56 10

Address: 4th arrondissement, 6 Parvis Notre-Dame - Pl. Jean-Paul II, 75004 Paris, France

Coordinates: 48.8530° N, 2.3498° E

Basilique du Sacre Coeur

Another of Paris's most popular museums, the Basilique du Sacre Coeur, which I have also presented in the previous chapter "Paris main attractions", is also for free. Sacre Coeur is located on the highest point of the city, at the top of Monmarte hill. Many people go to admire the fabulous view from its 271 foot high dome (82 meters), but even the view from the stairs or even below the stairs of the church is amazing, compensating for your effort to climb up there. Entrance to the basilica is free, but there's a fee in order to ascend onto the dome or explore the crypt.

Website: http://www.sacre-coeur-montmartre.com/

Tel: +33 1 53 41 89 00

Address: 18th arrondissement, 35 Rue du Chevalier de la Barre, 75018 Paris, France

Coordinates: 48.8867° N, 2.3430° E

Jardin du Luxembourg

The Jardin du Luxembourg is the second largest city park in Paris, and on a good day you might even spend the entire day wandering around and admiring its beauty. It was built in the 17th century and contains many monuments, statues and fountains, including the first model of the Statue of Liberty by Frederic Bartholdi. It is the perfect place to enjoy Paris's sun, read a book or have a picnic.

Address: 6th arrondissement, Rue de Medicis-Rue de Vaugirard, 75006 Paris, France

Phone: +33 1 42 34 23 62

Coordinates: 48.8469° N, 2.3372° E

Jardin des Tuileries

The Tuileries Garden is a historic public garden located between the Louvre and Place de la Concorde. It was first created by Catherine de Medici as the garden of the Tuileries Palace in 1564, but it was eventually opened to the public in 1667. In the 19th and 20th century, it was the place where Parisians celebrated, met, promenaded, and relaxed. It is a beautiful place to walk, take photos or just relax.

Address: 1starrondissement, 113 Rue de Rivoli, 75001 Paris, France

Coordinates: 48.8639° N, 2.3261° E

Pere Lachaise cemetery

Pere Lachaise cemetery is one of the most famous cemeteries in the world and probably the most haunting spot in Paris! Here you can visit the tombs of famous people like Edith Piaf, Oscar Wilde, Honore de Balzac, Marcel Proust, Yves Montand, Isadora Duncan and many others. Jim Morrison is also buried in this ancient cemetery. His grave is barricaded off to protect it from the thousands of his fans who come to visit. Georges Rodenbach's tomb features a bronze figure breaking out of the grave and Oscar Wilde's grave still has markings of the red lipstick by visitor's kisses.

Pere Lachaise cemetery has also one of the most atmospheric walks in Paris. One hundred acres of graves, memorials and tombs behind a looming stone entrance, tree-lined avenues and calling crows, create a unique, must-see scenery, which is visited by thousands of people each year.

Address: 20th arrondissement, 16 Rue du Repos, 75020 Paris, France

Phone: +33 1 55 25 82 10

Coordinates: 48.8600° N, 2.3960° E

Maison de Victor Hugo

Another popular free attraction is the city apartment of France's greatest 19th century romantic poet, Victor Hugo. Writer of "Les Miserables" in 1862, and "Notre-Dame de Paris" in 1831, Victor Hugo also produced more than 4,000 drawings. He is buried in the Pantheon, which means he is one of the great men of France, so visiting the place that he worked and lived might be a great experience for you, especially if you are a fan.

Address: 4th arrondissement, 6 Place des Vosges, 75004 Paris, France

Phone: +33 1 42 72 10 16

Coordinates: 48.8549° N, 2.3661° E

Jardin des Plantes

Jardin des Plantes is one of the world's oldest and largest botanical gardens. It was firstly opened to the public at 1640! Entrance is free except for the "menagerie" section specialized in the preservation of endangered species. You can see the small pandas though, since they can be clearly observed for free from the botanical gardens.

The garden is amazing and has plenty to offer to all ages. From playgrounds, ice-cream stalls and climb- up labyrinths, to tropical greenhouses and the old laboratory where Becquerel discovered radioactivity in 1896, Jardin des Plantes will surely satisfy even the most demanding visitor.

In the Musee National d' Histoire Naturelle, with its Grande Galerie de l' Evolution you or your children can admire the stuffed animals from all habitats, from marine species through the savannah jungle and Polar Regions. Also, the skeleton-filled museum of paleontology and anatomy and the spectacular collection of minerals are some quite interesting things to see.

Address: 5th arrondissement, 57 Rue Cuvier, 75005 Paris, France

Phone: +33 1 40 79 56 01

Coordinates: 48.8440° N, 2.3596° E

The Paris flower Market

The Paris flower market or "Le Marche aux Fleurs" is located on the Ile de la Cite near Pont Neuf. It is one of the oldest flower markets in the world, and was recently renamed to "Marche au fleurs reine Elizabeth II", after the visit of the Queen of Britain in 2014. It is a heaven of flowers, plants and trees, and Parisians have for centuries bought plants and flowers from here to decorate their houses and apartments. Primaveras, violets, orchids, bilberries, pomegranates and other exotic and beautiful plants are can be found here in this delightful place.

Many artists come here to relax, recharge their batteries and find inspiration for their next works. The enticing smells, vibrant colors and heavenly scenery are surely inspirational and relaxing. If you visit on Sunday, you will also have the chance to admire the Bird Market or "le Marche aux Oiseaux", where you can find rare species of birds and all the accessories to go with them.

Address: 4th arrondissement, Place Louis Lepine Quai de la Corse 75001 Paris, France

Phone: + 33 (0) 1 44 54 75 04

Coordinates: 48.855222 ° N, 2.347483° E

Fashion shows at Galeries Lafayette

Enjoying a fashion show is always welcome for most people, and in Paris you can enjoy the latest Galeries Lafayette's fashion collections for free. Every Friday afternoon Galeries Lafayette hosts a free fashion show, which involves professional models walking the runway and displaying the store's latest fashion collections. It would be a good idea to contact the store and confirm that the show will take place the date you are interested in attending, and possibly to book a seat.

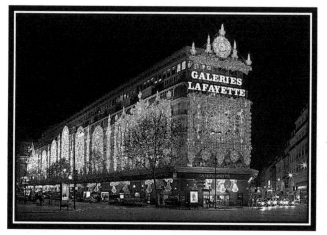

Address: 9th arrondissement, 40 Boulevard Haussmann, 75009, Paris, France

Phone: +33 0142 823025 or Email: fashionshow@galerieslafayette.com

Coordinates: 48.873572° N, 2.332095° E

Arenes de Lutece

The "Arenes de Lutece" is among the most important remains from the Gallo-Roman era in Paris. Dating back to 1 AD, this amphitheater is thought to be the longest Roman amphitheater ever constructed and could once seat 15,000 people. In the past it was used to present gladiatorial combats, while today it is being used for "petanque" games, which is a form of boules.

Address: 5th arrondissement, 49 Rue Monge, 75005 Paris, France

Phone: +33 1 45 35 02 56

Coordinates: 48.8450° N, 2.3528° E

Museums

In general, the permanent collections of museums owned and run by the City of Paris tend to be free, but you might be required to obtain a free ticket from the "Accueil" or ticket office before you can get in. Here are some of the best free Paris museums worth visiting:

- *Petit Palais* is an art museum run by the City of Paris. It has a large collection of great master's paintings including Rembrandt, Rubens, Monet, Nicolas Poussin, Gericault, Delacroix, Courbet, Monet and many more, plus a fine collection of artifacts. An excellent general collection museum and art gallery.
  Address: 8th arrondissement, Avenue Winston Churchill, 75008 Paris, France
  Phone: +33 1 53 43 40 00
  Website: http://www.petitpalais.paris.fr/
  Coordinates: 48.8450° N, 2.3528° E

- *City of Paris Museum of Modern Art* or "Musee d'Art Moderne de la Ville de Paris" is a major municipal museum dedicated to Modern and Contemporary art of the 20th and 21st centuries, and it has a large collection of late 19th, 20th and 21st century art, including works by Picasso, Bonnard, Bracque, Derain, Dufy, Modigliani, Rouault, Utrillo and many more.
  Address: 16th arrondissement, 11 Avenue du President Wilson, 75116 Paris, France
  Phone: + 33 (0)1 53 67 40 00
  Website: http://www.mam.paris.fr/
  Coordinates: 48.8644° N, 2.2973° E

- *Maison de Balzac* is a house museum in the former residence of French novelist Honore de Balzac (1799–1850), one of France's greatest 19th century novelists and playwrights. Balzac is regarded as one of the founders of realism in European literature and his writings influenced many subsequent novelists such as Marcel Proust, Emile Zola, Edgar Allan Poe, Charles Dickens, Anthony Trollope, Oscar Wilde, Eca de Queiros, Fyodor Dostoyevsky and many others.
  Address: 16th arrondissement, 47 Rue Raynouard, 75016 Paris, France
  Phone: +33 1 55 74 41 80
  Coordinates: 48.8553° N, 2.2808° E

- *The Carnavalet Museum or "Musee Carnavalet"* is dedicated to the history of the city of Paris. The exhibits inside the museum show the transformation of the village of Lutece, which was inhabited by the Parisii tribes, to the grand city of modern Paris. The museum has a large collection of exhibits which include about 2,600 paintings, 20,000 drawings, 300,000 engravings, 150,000 photographs, 2,000 modern sculptures and 800 pieces of furniture, thousands of ceramics and decorations, models, signs, coins, countless items, many of them souvenirs of famous characters, and thousands of archeological fragments.

Address: 3rd arrondissement, 16 Rue des Francs Bourgeois, 75003 Paris, France

Phone: +33 1 44 59 58 58

Website: http://www.carnavalet.paris.fr/

Coordinates: 48.8574° N, 2.3621° E

- The *Musee Cognacq-Jay* is a magnificent 16th century private residence (hotel particulier), with a collection of 18th century art, sculptures and crafts, about 1,200 in total. The museum's collection was formed between 1900–1925 by Theodore-Ernest Cognacq (1839–1928) and his wife Marie-Louise Jay (1838–1925). The collection emphasizes on 18th century France, ranging from European and Chinese ceramics, jewels, and snuffboxes, to paintings by Louis-Leopold Boilly, Francois Boucher, Canaletto, Jean-Simeon Chardin and many more. It is one of the 14 City of Paris' Museums that have been incorporated since 1 January 2013 in the public institution "Paris Musees".

  Address: 9th arrondissement, 8 Rue Elzevir, 75003 Paris, France

  Phone: +33 1 40 27 07 21

  Website: http://www.museecognacqjay.paris.fr/en

  Coordinates: 48.8582° N, 2.3614° E

- *The Museum of Romantic Life or "Musee de la Vie Romantique"* is mostly dedicated to two artists who were active during the Romantic era: writer George Sand and painter Ary Scheffer. In the first floor, the museum hosts numerous mementos of George Sand including family portraits, household possessions, pieces of jewelry and rare watercolors called "dendrites". On the second floor, you can admire a large number of Romantic canvases, sculptures and objects d'art, like portraits of Pauline Viardot and Queen Marie-Amelie, sculptures by Barre, Bartholdi, Antonin Moine and many more.

  Address: 9th arrondissement, 16 Rue Chaptal, 75009 Paris, France

  Phone: +33 (0)1 55 31 95 67

  Coordinates: 48.8809° N, 2.3334° E

- *Musee Bourdelle* is a small art museum built around Antoine Bourdelle's former studio and apartment with more than 500 works. The museum preserves the studio of sculptor Antoine Bourdelle (1861–1929), and provides an excellent example of Parisian ateliers from the late 19th and early 20th centuries, by capturing the spirit of Montparnasse when it was the center of the art world. Bourdelle's studio was active from 1885-1929, and he was an assistant of Rodin and teacher of Giacometti. He specialized in monumental sculptures, like the frieze for the Theatre des Champs-Elysees. Today the museum hosts various works including marble, plaster, and bronze statues, pastels, paintings, fresco sketches, and Bourdelle's personal collection of works by great artists including Eugene Delacroix, Eugene Carriere, Auguste Rodin, Jean Auguste Dominique Ingres and more. It also has document archives of Greek and medieval works.

Address: 15th arrondissement, 16-18 Rue Antoine Bourdelle, 75015 Paris, France

Phone: +33 1 49 54 73 73

Website: http://www.bourdelle.paris.fr/en

Coordinates: 48.8431° N, 2.3183° E

River Seine Cruises

Cruising along the Seine is one of those moments you will never forget in your entire life. You can choose to cruise either during daylight, in order to shoot the best photos of the Eiffel tower and the Louvre museum from the river, or to cruise in the evening and understand why this city is called "City of light"! Truly, the view of Paris from a cruise during the night is astonishing. Seeing the Eifel tower in front of you, its lights reflecting in the water, and its greatness of 986 feet in front of you, is something you will remember forever.

There are two types of cruises in the river Seine, and more than two companies offering such services; sightseeing and dinner (or brunch) cruises. Both of them follow a similar route from the Eiffel tower on one side and circling Ile Saint Louis on the other. Sightseeing cruises last for one hour, while dinner cruises last one or optionally up to two hours with extra charge. Of course prices are not comparable since sightseeing cruises only offer the service of boat ride at approximately 15 Euros per person. You can get better prices if you book online, as in most of Paris services and attractions. Dinner cruises might start at 60€ per person and up, and in most cases they offer full 3 course meals. Even if you choose a sightseeing cruise though, there is a canteen, from where you can buy food and drinks before starting the cruise. For example you can buy a glass of red wine, and enjoy it while admiring Paris from the Seine. Both cruise types offer guides in 2 languages, French and English.

Keep in mind that it might get chilly in the Seine even in mid-summer, especially at night, so be prepared. If you cruise in the spring or autumn you will surely need a coat. Ship owners adjust their ships by adding nylon covers in cold nights if the ship is open (mostly sightseeing cruises), but still you need to be prepared. Cruising the Seine with a cruise ship is a must if you are travelling to Paris, so be sure to include that in your planning.

Shopping

Paris is the shopping Mecca of the world, and the sensation of walking in the same city where the famous 19th century "grands magasins" (department stores) offered their posh products in the grands boulevards just makes you feel like living in a dream. You can feel this sensation even today, since Paris has a brilliant mix of boutiques that seem to have come out of a movie, but there are also markets and

mega stores that offer just about anything. Each arrondisment though has its own style, so you need to know where to go depending on what you want.

Le Marais is the center for casual wear and street fashion, as well as the place for people who fancy unique and finely-crafted products. Moreover, antique and art lovers will find their paradise in Place des Vosges. Rue des Francs-Bourgeois and Rue des Rosiers are the places to look for finely crafted jewelry. Le Marais is also a place to taste high quality tea after finishing shopping.

In contrast with Le Marais, *Boulevard Haussmann and the Grands Boulevards* are the places to travel back in time, and get lost to the prestigious and dazzling Belle-Epoque and its "grands magasins". Huge department stores like Galeries Lafayette and Printemps dominate Boulevard Haussmann with real Belle Epoque grandeur. Top designer's collections, gourmet food shopping and jewelry are only some of the goods you can buy here. Apart from the above, you will also find high-quality boutiques, some of them having collections of top designers like Jean-Paul Gaultier, and also old bookshops and old-fashioned toy shops. The main streets to focus are Boulevard Haussmann and Place de la Madeleine.

The Louvre area offers classic and elegant products in mainstream chains and shops, mostly on rue de Rivoli. The Faubourg Saint-Honore area is Paris's heart of design and fashion. The Saint-Honore fashion area is occupied by designers like Hermes, Versace, and Yves Saint Laurent, but also houses resolutely trendy concept shops. Elegant boutiques around the Palais Royal offer luxury perfumes, vintage items, jewelry and art. Also make sure you walk on Rue de la Paix and around Place Vendome.

The area around *Chatelet-les Halles* was transformed into a major shopping area in the 20th century, and you can find great bargains here. The much trendier Rue Montorgueil area houses quirky contemporary boutiques of young, cutting-edge designers. Make sure you walk Rue Pierre- Lescot, Rue Etienne Marcel and Rue de Turbigo.

In *St-Germain-des-Pres* you can find contemporary furniture, books, kitchen and design shops, all in chic and classical style. Furthermore, famous boutiques and a gourmet market can be found here. Don't forget to visit Rue Saint-Andre des Arts for rare books, gifts, and vintage threads. Blvd. St.-Germain, Rue St. Andre-des-Arts and Rue de Sevres are the main streets to walk here.

Champs-Elysees and Avenue Montaigne are the fashion centers of Paris, with legendary designers like Chanel and Dior lining the street with flagship boutiques at Avenue Montaigne. Champs-Elysees houses luxury big brands like Louis Vuitton as well as trendy global chains like Zara. This area is best for designer shopping, Sunday shopping and trendy chain stores.

Visiting *flea markets* in Paris might be a great experience mostly for antiques and odd items, as well as discounted and vintage clothes and shoes. The city's largest flea market takes place at Saint-Ouen, located at the very northern tip of Paris, and dates back to the 19th century.

There are also many more flea markets around the city, and they're pretty much all worth visiting. Just make sure you watch for pickpockets there.

In general, shops in Paris remain open from 10 a.m. to 7 p.m. and from Monday to Saturday, but larger stores usually stay open later on Thursdays. Smaller shops often (this is not a rule though) stay closed all day on Monday and sometimes for a couple of hours at lunchtime. Moreover, always take a receipt (ticket de caisse) when shopping, since it is impossible to return a product without it.

Useful apps

I know this is not an ordinary chapter for a guide, but since we are living in an era of technological advances, and smartphones are a part of our everyday life, why not exploit them to make our traveling easier and more fun as well? In this chapter I am suggesting some android and iOS applications that will make your vacation in Paris easier and more fun, even save you a lot of money. I am trying to suggest only free applications, or applications that offer useful functions for free, since advertising applications is not my intention. I am suggesting all the apps from personal experience, since I have used or keep using them myself.

Android Apps

TripAdvisor

This is a must have app during your travel to Paris, and as you understand it is the app of the known travel website Trip Advisor. In order to download data for Paris, you need to open "Trip Advisor sign in or signup" for free, and then choose the city you are interested in. Once you download the date, you can use the city map and many other features offline.

This app is great and let me explain what its most useful features are. First of all, once you download the data of the city, you can open the map and use it like being in Google maps (actually this is Google maps). You can zoom in, see street names, and if you enable your GPS, you will even see exactly where you are on the map! Most importantly you can do all that offline. It doesn't have navigation, but still you know where you are, and if you know where you want to go, it's pretty easy to do so. Another cool feature is that you can choose a neighborhood and the app will delimit it for you. So if you are wondering where the Latin Quarter is, just choose it, and the app will show you exactly where it starts and where it ends. If you combine this with the GPS function, you will know if you are in the Latin Quarter or not.

Another cool feature is that it can show the attractions on the map, so you will know when you are close to one. You can even set your own landmarks, which show as a star, and this way you can create your own daily schedule. Except from attractions, there are other categories that can show on the map. Food& Drink, Hotels, Nightlife, Shopping, Tickets/Tours/ Metro Stations, ATMs can all show on the map in order for you to find them easily. If you can't imagine how useful this is, let me give you an example: Let's assume you are walking in the streets of Paris for some 4 hours, have seen some great attractions, but now you are really hungry and want to taste French cuisine. You run this app, and choose to open Food & Drink category on the map. Since you also have the GPS enabled the app shows your position on the map and all available food related stores near you. Furthermore, since Paris offers free internet connection almost all over the city center, you can even choose a restaurant near you, and see Trip Advisor people reviews and star score for it! In many cases people even mention prices along with their reviews. So in 5 minutes, you know more about this restaurant than a Parisian that lives in the next block! It's that simple. And most importantly, this app is totally free.

Android app link:

https://play.google.com/store/apps/details?id=com.tripadvisor.tripadvisor&hl=en

iOS app link:

https://itunes.apple.com/gr/app/tripadvisor-hotels-flights/id284876795?mt=8

Happy Hours Paris

This is an incredible little app made by an amateur local Frenchman, which shows where you can find Bars and Restaurants with Happy Hour in Paris. For those of you who don't know what "Happy hour" is, it is specific hours of the day that a store offers drinks in lower prices than usual. So, this app might spare you a lot of money in drinks, since you will exactly know which stores have happy hours, which hours, and the prices of the drinks.

If you are connected to the internet, this app will show all stores that currently have happy hours on the map, and will even show prices, for example "beer pint 4€" or "Cocktail 5€" depending on what the store offers. You can zoom in and out of the map, since this is Google maps as well. There is a different icon for beer and different for cocktail, and stores offering both in Happy Hour have both icons on them. If you don't have internet connection, the app shows the stores only in a list and not on the map, which is less, but still useful.

The amazing thing about this app is that it even has searching filters! You can search stores with Happy hour and one of the following filter: Maximum beer-cocktail-champagne price, maximum distance from current position, day of the week and hour of the day. So for example, when you sit for a coffee in the afternoon, you might search for bars that have happy hour during 20:00 and 22:00 with maximum cocktail price of 6€ within 2 km radius from your current position. There might be a bar with a happy hour next to the one you are heading, so run the app first! If you don't know if the bar is good, open Trip Advisor app and read reviews! You have the power in your hands, and more specifically in your....smartphone!

This app is free and available only for Andoid:

https://play.google.com/store/apps/details?id=com.camdentom.happyhours

Visit Paris by Metro – RATP

You got the app to take you to the attractions during the day, you got the app to take you for a drink during the night, now the only thing that is missing is how to get there. Well, this is exactly what this app is doing. It is an app created by the RATP, which operates metro, rail, tramway and bus services in Paris. The app is 100% free and offers very useful functions. It is fully translated into English, German, Dutch, Italian, Spanish, Japanese, Chinese, Brazilian, Portuguese and Russian,

First of all there is a metro map available in your mobile phone at all times. You can easily see at which stop you are and how to go to the one you want. The most amazing function though, is that you can enter 2 points, like Louvre to Eiffel tower, if you are in the Louvre and want to go to the Eiffel Tower by metro, and the app calculates automatically and shows what metro lines you must use to go to your destination and the time in minutes to get there! It creates a custom itinerary for you, and automatically shows what means of transportation you need to use, even if more than one is included. So, if an itinerary includes metro-bus-metro the app will automatically show that. This is your ultimate app on Paris transportation, and it is for free.

It also has information on ticket and unlimited travel passes prices and there is a Google map available here as well, even offline if you download it.

Android app link:

https://play.google.com/store/apps/details?id=net.ixxi.ratp.tourisme

iOS app link:

https://itunes.apple.com/gr/app/visit-paris-by-metro-ratp/id660175477?mt=8

Toilets in Paris

Paris has more than 400 free public toilets all over the city, "Les sanisettes". They are well maintained and self-cleaning and of course very useful to tourists that might be walking around Paris all day. What's cooler though, is that there is an app that can find the public toilet closest to you! The app needs internet connection to show the toilets on the map (Google maps), which won't be a problem since there is free internet connection almost in all parts of Paris's center. Even if you are in a part that there is no internet connection, the app offers a list of toilets and their address.

The app offers more functions than just show the toilets on the map. It can find the closest toilet to your current position by choosing the option "Around me". It can also find all toilets in a specific address, and of course all toilets in Paris. That's it. Simple and very useful app, and most importantly absolutely free. This app is only available in Android, but there is a similar app for iOS from another developer. The strong point of the iOS app is that it can work offline.

Android app link:

https://play.google.com/store/apps/details?id=com.magetys.sanisettes

iOS similar App link:

https://itunes.apple.com/gr/app/public-toilets-in-paris-offline/id882340250?mt=8

iOS Apps

TripAdvisor

Please see analysis in the Android section of this chapter just above.

iOS app link:

https://itunes.apple.com/gr/app/tripadvisor-hotels-flights/id284876795?mt=8

Visit Paris by Metro – RATP

Please see analysis in the Android section of this chapter just above.

iOS app link:

https://itunes.apple.com/gr/app/visit-paris-by-metro-ratp/id660175477?mt=8

Public Toilets In Paris Offline

Please see analysis in the Android section of this chapter just above.

iOS app link:

https://itunes.apple.com/gr/app/public-toilets-in-paris-offline/id882340250?mt=8

Hidden Paris

This is a great app for those of you that will stay in Paris long enough to see all major attractions, and want to discover some hidden gems. It has 13 unusual and intriguing places to visit in Paris. It has photos of the secret place, information on what it is and its history, and some more practical information like: arrondisment, address, phone, entrance (free or price), open hours, closest metro station and web page. It's a fun little app, but I would use it only after I have seen at least the major attractions in Paris. The app is free for some of the attractions, but you must pay 2.99 € for more.

iOS app link:

https://itunes.apple.com/gr/app/hidden-paris/id429451466?mt=8

Detailed Itinerary

Making an itinerary for Paris is not an easy task. It is a city with so many things to see that is nearly impossible to fit them all in your schedule. The good news though is that the vast majority of must-see attractions are located in the city center, so you don't need to travel a lot, plus Paris has a great transportation system, which will allow you to move from one part of the city center to another quickly and easily. With good planning, you will be able to fit most attractions in your schedule, but of course the attractions you will be able to see, and how tight the schedule will be depends on how many days you plan to stay in the City of Light. The more days, the more things you will be able to see.

In this chapter you will find a detailed itinerary, which will help you plan your trip smartly and exploit as much of Paris as you can. Remember that you can find information on most of the attractions mentioned in the itinerary, in the chapters "Paris Main Attractions" and "Free Attractions". The basic itinerary is for 5 days, but there is also an extension for another 2 days, and you can adjust your schedule depending on how many days you will stay. If you are going to stay more than 7 days, you can just loosen the schedule and visit less places per day, since it is a bit tight, or visit some extra places and attractions that you have seen in previous chapters of this guide. Of course, strolling around Paris's beautiful streets without any planning at all, might be even more fun, if you can spare a day or two. This itinerary has a very useful interactive route map accompanying it. You can find more information in chapter "Paris download zone".

DAY 1

Forms of transportation needed: Walking

1. **Tour Eiffel (Eiffel Tower):** Day one starts with Paris's most known attraction, the Eiffel Tower. Be sure to get there early, especially in the summer, since long queues are to be expected. 09:00 is a good time to begin your first day of adventure in Paris.
2. **Champ de Mars (Field of Mars):** When leaving the Eiffel Tower (or when arriving, it's up to you), don't forget to admire Champ de Mars, which means "Field of Mars", the beautiful greenspace located just in front of the Eiffel Tower.
3. **Hotel National des Invalides (The National Residence of the Invalids):** After relaxing in Champ de Mars, walk to Hotel National des

Invalides to admire Napoleon's eternal resting place. Don't forget that next to it there is the arm's museum, which contains an extensive collection of military artifacts, thus you will probably spend much more time in it than in Napoleon's tomb.

4. **Palais Bourbon:** Next stop, Palais Bourbon, an impressive palace that today serves as the seat of the French National Assembly, the lower legislative chamber of the French government. You can take individual or guided tours if you want, walk around this fascinating building, and admire its beautiful architecture.

5. **Pont Alexander III:** Pont Alexander III bridge is widely regarded as the most ornate, extravagant bridge of Paris, and is classified as a French historic monument. Grab the opportunity to take some lovely photos with the river Seine and Eiffel Tower in the background!

6. **Musee des Egouts de Paris (Paris Sewer Museum):** The Paris Sewer Museum is a history museum located in the sewers at the esplanade Habib-Bourguiba. It is a strange tourist attraction, which gives you a different perspective of the city. A self-guided tour is available, but be warned that there is a distinctive smell, as these are real working sewers of Paris, so you may want to skip this attraction if you don't like the idea. I must warn you though that it is quite interesting in a grotesque way.

7. **Trocadero:** The final stop for your first day is the Trocadero area. Trocadero offers the best view of the Eifel Tower, better than any other in Paris. For that reason you will see dozens of people with their cameras in hand, trying to shoot the perfect photograph of the tower, especially at the start of every hour, when the tower lights sparkle for 5 minutes. If you want to do the same, don't forget to bring your tripod with you! You can sit on the grass and enjoy a beer, like many people do, or choose one of the bar-restaurants behind the square to relax and enjoy a meal or just a glass of French wine while admiring the Tower. What better way to end the first day of your Paris trip? It's just magical.

DAY 2

Forms of transportation needed: Walking, Metro (Optional)

1. **Louvre Museum:** I guess you already know what the Louvre Museum is, it's one of the world's largest museums and a historic monument of Paris. This means that, except of its vast and stunning artifact collection, the building itself is interesting, since it is an old Palace and Fortress. If you want to carefully examine all the collections of the museum, you will probably need at least 2-3 days, so it is best to make a decision; either spend one whole day in Louvre and

re-schedule the rest attractions of the day, or choose specific parts of the museum to visit. A quick visit to, say, half the museum without spending more than 2-3 minutes in each artifact, will take you about 4-5 hours. So the best thing to do is go to ultimateurbanguides.com, click on "Download Zones" – "Paris Download Zone", enter the code "uugfr33zone" without the "" and download the Louvre Museum Plan and Information, where you will find a detailed floor plan of the museum, which will help you program your visit to Louvre efficiently.

2. **Hotel de Ville (City Hall):** Next stop after the Louvre Museum is the Hotel de Ville. It is best to go there by foot, since it is not too far and it is a nice walk across the Seine, but if you want you can use the Metro (it's only one stop away). Take metro line 1 from Louvre-Rivoli towards Chateau de Vincennes and get off at Hotel de Ville stop. Hotel de Ville has a great architecture, and will amaze you, especially if you visit it during Christmas time. It is a must-see attraction in Paris.

3. **Marche aux Fleurs - Reine Elizabeth II (Flower Market):** Very close to Hotel de Ville, on Isle de la Cite, you will find Paris's most known Flower market. You won't spend much time here, except if you want to relax a bit with the heady aromas of the flowers.

4. **Sainte-Chapelle (Holy Chapel):** Merely a block away of the flower market you will find Sainte-Chapelle, a spectacular hidden Chapel. Expect long queues, so be prepared.

5. **Cathedrale Notre-Dame de Paris (Notre-Dame Cathedral):** Final stop for Day 2, the famous Notre-Dame Cathedral. If you spent too much time in the Louvre museum, you might want to change this day's schedule and move the visit to Notre-Dame earlier than Sainte-Chapelle or even Marche aux Fleurs, since after 17:30 the south tower is closed to visitors. After visiting the Cathedral, you can have a romantic night cruise on Seine or just relax having a drink in one of the bars located on the other side of the Seine, in Quai de Montebello Avenue, with an amazing view of Notre-Dame Cathedral at night.

DAY 3

Forms of transportation needed: Train/Bus/Car

1. **Pont Neuf (Paris zero point):** Day 3 is entirely dedicated to visiting the Chateau de Versailles. Pont Neuf is just a reference point on where to start your route to Versailles. Depending on where you are staying in Paris, another point in the city might be more suitable for you. Here are the alternatives to get to Versailles:

- **By Train: RER C** - To get to the palace of Versailles, make sure to buy a ticket to "Versailles Rive Gauche" or a Navigo, Mobilis or Paris Visit pass zones 1-4 (t+ ticket is not valid for this journey).
  SNCF Trains
  Arrive at Versailles Chantiers station from Paris Montparnasse. Interactive map is available at
  http://bienvenue.chateauversailles.fr/en/overview/train-stations#!panel-0-subpanel-0
  Arrive at Versailles Rive Droite station from Paris Saint Lazare. Interactive map is available at
  http://bienvenue.chateauversailles.fr/en/overview/train-stations#!panel-0-subpanel-2
  Train schedule on www.transilien.com
- **By Coach Versailles Express:** Versailles Express offers transfers to the Palace of Versailles from the Eiffel Tower in Paris. From Tuesday to Sunday they offer two departures per day at 8 a.m. (back at 12:30) and 2 p.m. (back at 6 p.m.).Transfer from Paris with a pickup in Port de la Bourdonnais (Parking of Bateaux Parisiens, right below the Eiffel Tower). You can verify routes and book a ticket at www.versaillesexpress.com
- **By car:** You can also drive to the Palace, just take A13 motorway and look for exit "Versailles Centre". Paying car parks are available at the Place d' Armes, Allee de Bailly, Grand Trianon and Petit Trianon.
  If you are using a GPS device, just input the following coordinates of the Palace of Versailles:
  48°48'17N
  2°07'15E
2. **Chateau de Versailles (Palace of Versailles):** The Chateau de Versailles, as we have seen in "Paris main Attraction" chapter of this book, is a must-see Paris attraction, which will take a whole day for you to see and explore, since it is located almost 20 km from Paris, and both the Palace/Chateau and Gardens are on a massive scale. Food and coffee are available there in reasonable prices. Also, audio guides are available for extra cost.

DAY 4

Forms of transportation needed: Walking, Metro

1. **Palais Garnier (Opera House):** Palais Garnier, one of the most known Opera houses in the world, with its exquisite interior and exterior, is a

must-see attraction in Paris. It is open for visitors, and a self-guided tour is available, as well as organized tours, which are advised to book before getting there. If you want to fully experience its greatness though, it is best to be there for a performance. After the Opera, you can walk on the "Avenue de l' Opera" and admire the amazing architecture of Paris.

2. **Jardin des Tuileries (Tuileries Garden):** This is one of the most beautiful Parisian parks. You can spend as little as 15 minutes here, just to take some great photos, or relax a little longer, hearing the birds and watching the amazing scenery. Be warned though that dozens of tourists wander here all day, so don't expect a quiet place.

3. **Place de la Concorde:** The Place de la Concorde is the largest square in the French capital. It is also the start of the famous Champs-Elysees avenue. After finishing with taking photos on the square, make sure you continue towards Champs-Elysees.

4. **Petit Palais (Small Palace):** Petit Palais houses the City of Paris Museum of Fine Arts. The building itself is very beautiful, and worth the visit just to see its architecture, even if you don't plan to visit the museum. The permanent collection is free, and it shouldn't take more than an hour if you see all exhibits. Note that there is no English translation on the explanations.

5. **Grand Palais (Grand Palace):** Grand Palais is just accross Petit Palais, and it houses major art exhibits and cultural events, including a science museum, the "Palais de la Decouverte". Most likely you will find long queues here, so be prepared if you are planning on visiting the museum.

6. **Arc de Triomphe de l'Etoile (Triumphal Arch of the Star):** At the end of the magnificent Champs-Elysees avenue, you will find the famous Arc de Triomphe. Underground tunnels will allow you to access the monument safely. If you want to climb up to the arc you have to purchase a ticket. The visit to the Arc shouldn't take more than 30 minutes. After that you need to use the metro to go to Monmarte and visit Sacre-Coeur. From "Charles de Gaul Etoile" metro station located right below the Arc, take metro line 2 towards "Nation". You need to get off at "Pigalle".

7. **Sacre-Coeur Basilica (The Basilica of the Sacred Heart of Paris):** Walk up towards Sacre Coeur and enjoy the lovely roads filled with souvenir shops. If you don't want to walk all the way up, there is a furniculaire available for the price of one metro ticket. Visiting the Basilica is free. You definitely have to wander on the streets of Monmarte behind the church, to see the picturesque scenery and the street artists. This day can end with a glass of red wine in the bohemian part of Paris, the lovely Monmarte.

DAY 5

Forms of transportation needed: Walking

1. **Jardin du Luxembourg (Luxembourg Gardens):** This day starts with a walk in the beautiful Luxembourg Gardens, a real peaceful setting in this bustling city. Take a walk there and enjoy the beautiful scenery.
2. **Musee national du Moyen Age (National Museum of the Middle Ages) former Musee de Cluny:** Next stop is the national museum of the middle Ages, which is the most outstanding example still extant of civic architecture in medieval Paris. It combines Gothic and Renaissance elements in an amazing building which travels you back in time. You will spend about 1.5 hours here.
3. **Sorbonne:** Opposite the museum you will see the famous Sorbonne University, oozing character and intellect. Enjoy the charming architecture before proceeding to your next stop, the Pantheon.
4. **Pantheon:** Not far away from the Sorbonne University you will find the Pantheon. Like most Paris's attractions, you can buy tickets in advance to skip long queues. Don't forget to visit the underground tomb.
5. **Jardin des Plantes (Botanical garden):** After a small walk in the Parisian roads you will find yourself in the last stop of today's journey, the Jardin des Plantes, the main botanical garden in Paris. As we have mentioned, Jardin des Plantes has many things to offer to all ages, so spend as much time as you want here. The best thing to do though, is to dedicate a reasonable amount of time here and then just wander around the Latin Quarter, feel the lively atmosphere and enjoy a moderately priced simple French meal, in one of the dozen bistros located here.

EXTRA DAYS

DAY 6

Forms of transportation needed: Walking, Metro

1. **Forum des Halles:** Les Halles was the traditional central market of Paris where for hundreds of year merchants came from all over to sell their goods. It was demolished in 1971 and replaced with the Forum des Halles, a modern shopping mall with dozens of stores, coffee houses, restaurants etc, most of them being overpriced though.

2. **The Centre Pompidou:** Centre Pompidou is a postmodern/high tech building which is interesting to see for its architecture. It houses a vast public library, the largest museum of modern art in Europe and a center for music and acoustic research. Also, you can have lunch or dinner at its impressive top floor restaurant that overlooks the city. Reservation might be needed, at least for dinner.

3. **Pere Lachaise Cemetery:** It's quite a distance from Pompidou to the Pere Lachaise Cemetery so it is better to use metro. Take metro line 11 from "Rambuteau" towards "Mairie des Lilas". Then, at "Repiblique", change to line 3 towards "Gallieni" and get off at "Pere Lachaise". It is best to visit Pere Lachaise before the other attractions of the day (especially if you are there when the days are small), because you want to explore some of the most famous graves in daytime.

4. **Maison de Victor Hugo (House of Victor Hugo):** You will again need to use the metro to go to the House of Victor Hugo. Again use line 3, but now towards "Pont de Levallois Becon", and at "Republique" change to line 5 towards "Place D' Italie". You need to get off at "Bastille". It is definitely worth visiting the house of Victor Hugo, this free museum located in a picturesque and historic square. You will spend about 15-25 minutes to see this small museum. There is a ticket for the exhibit and for the audio guide.

5. **Place de la Bastille:** Don't expect to see anything special or eye-catching in Place de la Bastille, since it is just a normal lovely square. It is the historical significance of this square that it makes it worth visiting. This is where the Bastille prison stood until the 'Storming of the Bastille' and its subsequent physical destruction between 14 July 1789 and 14 July 1790, during the French Revolution. Today you can see the "July Column" in the center of the square, plus it has many cafes, bars, night clubs, and concert halls around it, where you can enjoy your coffee or drink and relax.

DAY 7

Forms of transportation needed: Train/Bus/Car

1. **Pont Neuf:** Day 7 is entirely dedicated to visiting Disneyland. Pont Neuf is just a reference point on where to start your route to Disneyland. Depending on where you are staying in Paris, another point in the city might be more suitable for you. Disneyland Paris is 32 km or 20 miles away from Paris. To make your way to Disneyland Paris from the city center, you have to access Line A of the city's suburban train network, the RER. You can access the RER from the following Paris stations: Charles de Gaulle

Etoile, Auberer, Chatelet Les Halles, Gare de Lyon and Nation. Once there you must take line A4, which will take you to Disneyland Paris. Visit my website www.uuguides.com to download for free a map of the RER network of Paris, from the Paris download zone (see chapter "Paris download zone"). Alternatively, you can drive if you have a car. The coordinates to Disneyland Paris are 48.8687° N, 2.7818° E.

2. **Disneyland Paris:** Disneyland Paris is the most visited theme park in all of Europe, and it will keep you occupied for the whole day, even more than one day! Thus day seven is entirely dedicated to Disneyland Paris. Disneyland Paris can offer everything that you will need for the whole day, which is food, drink and lots of fun! Long queues should be expected, so you can buy your tickets in advance.

Important things to know

Here you can find some useful travel tips everyone should know before visiting Paris.

- The standard French look is dressier than the American equivalent. Don't wear athletic clothes, at least during your night out. Neat jeans are acceptable everywhere, except at more chic restaurants, which may have a dress code.
- Try to behave a bit formal, since informal American-style manners are considered impolite. Speaking French by using the phrasebook of this guide will help you a lot with establishing good relationships with the locals.
- It is customary in French culture to greet people as you enter and exit stores, so be sure to do that using the words and phrases included in the phrasebook.
- Men can stare at a woman and admire her even after eye-contact. This is not weird nor should it offend you.
- One third of all French are smokers, so if you are not a smoker prepare yourself. Smoking though is prohibited in closed public places like restaurants or cafes.
- In France the first floor is the floor above the ground floor (rez-de-chaussee).
- France is a member of the Eurozone, so its national currency is the Euro (EUR) or €.
- Stick to the ATMs for the best exchange rates since exchanging cash at your hotel or in a store is never going to be to your advantage.
- In restaurants, when you're ready for the check, you must ask for it because it is considered rude to bring a bill unbidden. In cafes you will get a register receipt with your order.
- There is no rule for tipping in France and bills by law include service cost, so you are not required to leave a tip. It is polite though to round your bill and leave a tip of about 0.30€ for a beer up to 3€ for a meal or other services and 5% of the meal value in expensive restaurants.
- If you order a simple cafe, you'll get an espresso-like shot in a small cup. If you want a milky coffee akin to a latte, order a cafe creme.
- Cabs are really expensive in Paris, so use public transport when possible. Metro is the best solution, since it is easy to master and it covers all places a tourist might need to go to.

- Paris has a wide network of free Wi-Fi, which will keep you connected in most places that you will go, at least in Paris town center.
- Paris has more than 400 free public toilettes all over the city. They are well maintained and self-cleaning.
- All citizens of Canada and the United States, even infants, need a valid passport to enter France for stays of up to 90 days.
- The electrical current in Paris is 220 volts, 50 AC, and the 2 round two-pin plugs are used. Visitors from North America are required to have a transformer and British visitors an adaptor. Some hotels actually provide these adaptors, but you can also buy them from most stores with electrical equipment, or even at the airport.
- Emergency contacts in France: Police: 112, 17. Ambulance: 15. Fire department: 18. General emergency services for police, fire, and ambulance (like 911): 112.

Paris free Download Zone

Paris download zone is a password protected part of our website www.uuguides.com, with exclusive content only accessible to buyers of this book. It contains useful material that can be used to make your trip to Paris easier and more fun. The content is dynamic, which means we try to enrich it and keep existing content updated.

In order to access "Paris Download Zone", go to www.uuguides.com and press "Paris download zone" under menu "Download zones". After that, you will need to enter the password "uugfr33zone" (without the quote marks) to gain access.

The main thing that you will find is the interactive route map and detailed instructions on how to use it. Except from that, there are plenty of maps for you to download, save as .pdf (popular file format) in your computer, or print. Map of Paris, map of the metro and train system and Louvre plan information are only some of them.

In case you have any kind of problem using the content or accessing Paris download zone, you can contact us through the contact page of our website www.uuguides.com.

French Phrasebook

This book offers everything one would need during a trip in Paris. Someone would say that the only thing not incorporated in this book or in our website's exclusive content is a French phrasebook, for those of you that would like to blend in with the locals, impress them, and complete the romantic experience of visiting Paris with the appropriate words as well.

Our local linguistic experts have created a complete French phrasebook with more than 350 words and phrases that you will need during your trip to France. The phrases are organised in various categories to help you access the phrase you need quickly and easily. The categories are: Common signs, Basic Communication and Greetings, Numbers, Clock/Time, Days, Colors, Transportation/Directions, Shopping, Food/Drink and Emergency. This book is being sold for $2.99 in electronic form and $6.99 in printed, but we have decided to offer it to buyers of our Paris guide for free.

If you truly liked the guide you are reading, and you would like to share this opinion with others by posting a review to the store you bought this book from, we will be happy to compensate you for your time and your confidence to us by sending you the French phrasebook for free. For example, if you bought the book from Amazon.com, the procedure would be the following:

1. Go to the store that you bought the book from, e.g. Amazon.com, and post a 4 or 5 star positive review on our book. Sincerely write the reasons you liked the book, and how it helped you in your trip to Paris, or in learning about Paris. The comment must come from a verified purchase. For example, if you have purchased the book from Amazon, and you write the review using the same account, the purchase will automatically be verified.
2. Go to www.uuguides.com, click contact, complete the required fields, and select "I am interested in the free French phrasebook" in the field "Please choose how we can help you?"
3. In the comments of the contact page write "My name is Cathryn Sparks (replace with your name) and "I have bought the ultimate Paris guide from Amazon.com". My Amazon.com nickname is "Cathryn.Sparks" (replace with the name that is visible when you comment and post reviews on the store that you bought the book from) and I have just commented positively on your eBook at website www.amazon.com. Please send me my free French phrasebook".

4. After verifying your review, we will email you the French phrasebook in .pdf format and written permission to print the book one time for your own use. Make sure to check your spam folder as well in case your email provider falsely lists our email address as spam.

Please note that in no case we want you to post a positive review if you did not like our book. In that case, we urge you to contact us and explain why you did not like the book. We carefully listen to our readers in order to improve future editions of our books.

Connect with Cathryn

I would like to thank you for choosing my ultimate urban guide for Paris. As I say to my colleagues from all over the world, "feedback is gold", so I would be very happy to hear back from you. You can contact me by using the contact form at www.uuguides.com (alternatively www.ultimateurbanguides.wordpress.com) or email me at info@uuguides.com or xpressepublishing@gmail.com. Also, don't forget to follow my blog at www.uuguides.com (scroll down and input your email address), as well as my Facebook page www.facebook.com/uuguides, for receiving exclusive offers and updated information on Paris and many other cities of the world!

Be sure to keep my guide with you at all times during your trip to Paris, and have a great time at the most romantic city you will ever be, the City of Light, Paris.